AF324243

ARTHURIAN AND KNIGHTLY ART FROM THE MIDDLE AGES

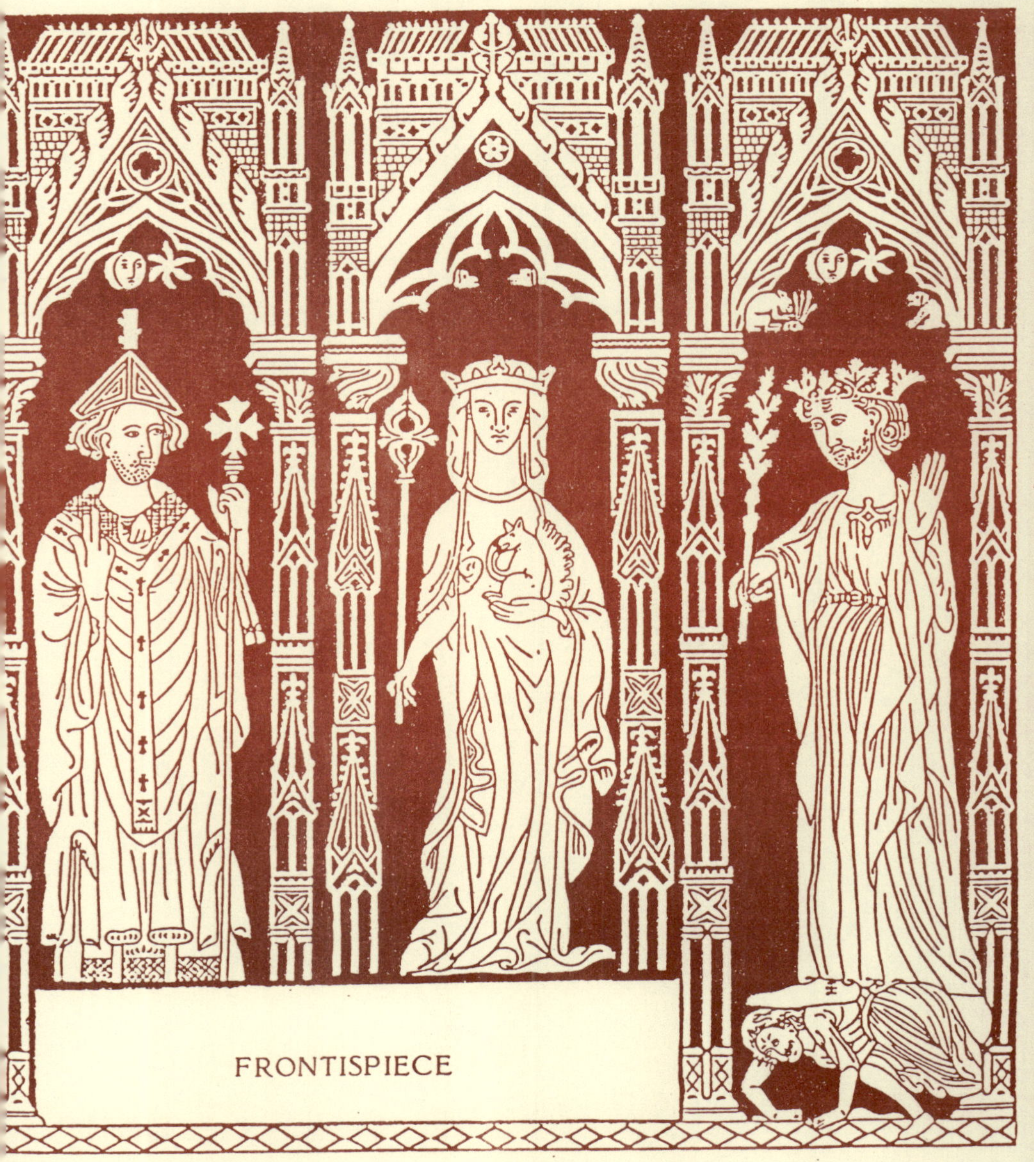

FRONTISPIECE

ACKNOWLEDGMENTS

The editor wishes to thank
Paul Larkin, Jane Sedge, Chertsey Museum,
and John Leb
for assistance in the preparation
of this book.

ARTHURIAN AND KNIGHTLY ART FROM THE MIDDLE AGES

By MANWARING SHURLOCK

Edited by DEREK BRYCE

Restored designs by JOHN LEB

LLANERCH ENTERPRISES,
Felinfach, Lampeter,
Dyfed SA48 8PJ.

ISBN 0947992278

CONTENTS

Text:

Plates:

CONTENTS

CONTENTS

EDITOR'S PREFACE

I have changed the title of Dr. Manwaring Shurlock's book from TILES FROM CHERTSEY ABBEY to ARTHURIAN AND KNIGHTLY ART FROM THE MIDDLE AGES to give a clearer idea of the contents, and also because some of the designs were taken from tiles found at Hales-Owen Abbey, near Birmingham, as well as from Chertsey in Surrey.

In editing the book, I have kept much of Dr. Shurlock's text unchanged, abridging here and there in the interest of conciseness; summarising some of the letters from his contemporaries which were printed in their entirety. I have also slightly abridged Baron de Cosson's notes on armour, retaining the most important points. I apologise to any readers who may think I have left out something that they consider important. Dr Shurlock's book was very large, with a page size of almost twelve inches by eighteen, which would have been very costly to reproduce in facsimile. By slightly abridging the text, and reducing the drawings by 50% linear, I have produced a book of normal dimensions and price.

The illustrations are taken from the original work, but some of them are presented as artist's restorations, where the missing fragments could be filled in with some confidence. A few of the imperfect drawings are left incomplete because of uncertainty as to what should be there. In the the case of restored drawings, I have included a miniature of Dr Shurlock's original as an inset.

Finally, I must add that I have not included Dr. Shurlock's personal comments, which reflected the attitudes of his time. He saw 'Tristram' as highly immoral, whereas he considered the poem on King Richard as amusing. Today's readers will not be shocked by Tristram, whereas they might well find the poet's fiction of King Richard's cannibalism offensive; black humour, racist, and in bad taste.

ARTHURIAN AND KNIGHTLY ART FROM THE MIDDLE AGES

BEING AN ACCOUNT OF THE REMARKABLE PAVEMENT TILES FROM CHERTSEY ABBEY, SURREY, AND HALESOWEN ABBEY, NEAR BIRMINGHAM.

Encaustic tiles were generally adopted by the architects and builders of the Middle Ages to form the pavements of churches throughout our native country and some parts of France, especially Normandy. The earliest apparently belonged to the latter part of the twelfth century, but it appears from the excellence of the manufacture, the quality of the remains, and the beauty of the designs, that the culminating point of excellence and popularity was reached during the thirteenth. Examples have been found in all parts of England, but the most admirable in point of manufacture are those of Chertsey Abbey, some of which were also used at Hales-Owen Abbey. The next beautiful form the pavement of the Chapter House at Westminster; and those of Salisbury are very fine.

The ancient process of manufacture of these tiles, appears to have been somewhat as follows:-

The moist clay, having been well-beaten, was compressed into the requisite shapes and thickness. These were probably exposed to the sun until they had acquired the proper degree of plasticity to retain any design impressed upon them by a stamp, so formed as to indent the ornamental pattern upon the face of the tile. The indented pattern was then filled up with a different coloured clay, which was usually pipe or other white clay. After the tiles were put into the furnace, a thin coating of powdered lead ore, mixed with clean sand, was probably dusted over the surfaces, so as to give a vitreous glaze when withdrawn from the kiln, which gave permanence, and added to the richness of the effect. The glaze gave the white clay a slight tinge of yellow, and added fulness of tone to the red colour which usually formed the ground upon which the pattern was relieved.

For the success of this simple operation it was necessary that the two kinds of clay employed should be of similar quality, for if in the furnace the white was liable to shrink more than the red, the work would be full of cracks; in the opposite case, the design would bulge and be thrown upwards. "Wasters" or spoilt tiles have been found on the sites of some ancient kilns, affording examples of both imperfections.

The tiles represented in this book are from fragments of a very remarkable pavement, which once formed the floors at Chertsey Abbey, and also Hales-Owen Abbey.

It is somewhat singular that, although the destruction of the vast, richly-endowed Chertsey Abbey, of which the pavement no doubt formed a grand feature, was so complete that scarcely one stone was allowed to remain on another, or a decorated tile to escape mutilation, no record has yet been found of the time when this destruction took place, under whose authority it occurred, or of any of the circumstances attending it.

The earliest mention of Chertsey Abbey is in the seventh century: Bede, in his 'Ecclesiastical History' describes it as a Monastery erected at 'Ceroti Insula' (Chertsey). This Ceroti Insula was subject to the over-lordship of Mercia, which was converted to Christianity about the middle of that century.

It appears from documents purporting to be the deeds of foundation, that in A.D. 666, Frithwold Sub-King or Viceroy of the Surrey-folk under Wulphere, King of Mercia, built the Monastery, in conjunction with Earconwald, afterwards Bishop of London, who ruled over it as its first Abbot.

In the ninth century the Abbey suffered from the incursions of the Danes. On one occasion the Abbot Beocca, a priest named Ethor, and ninety of the monks are said to have been slaughtered, and all the buildings, probably of wood, burnt.

The Monastery was re-built by Eodgar, A.D. 964, and assigned by him to the Benedictines at the instance of Dunstan, who was of the order. The first Benedictine Abbot was Ordbright.

The building of a new Monastery, in 1110, under Hugh, Abbot of Winchester, the election of John de Medmenham as Abbot in 1261, and of his successor, Bartholomew de Winchester in 1272, bring down the history of the Abbey to the year 1307, when its lasting prosperity was secured by the appointment of John de Rutherwyke, who is spoken of as "a most religious father, and a most prudent and profitable lord;" and in a commemorative stone at the east end of Great Bookham Church, he is described as "the venerable Abbot, who might be termed the convent's second founder, the restorer of all really good works, and the substantial improver of the manors belonging to the Monastery."

John de Rutherwyke ruled over the Abbey until the time of his death, in 1346, a period of 39 years, during which he was constantly engaged in building, repairing, and planting in various parts of the possessions of the Monastery. He erected new chancels to the Churches of Great Bookham and Egham, and restored the chancel at Epsom.

I visited the Public Record Office and examined the fine chartulery of Chertsey Abbey preserved there, with the hope of finding some account of the manufacture and laying of the tile pavement, but was disappointed, as previous to the time of John de Rutherwyke no account exists respecting the buildings of the Abbey.

In 1341 Edward III visited Chertsey Abbey, with

his court, and he appears to have shown special favour towards the Abbot and the religious community.

During the Abbacy of John May, no less an event took place than the internment within the walls of the Abbey of one of England's kings. In 1471 Henry VI, who had been dethroned ten years before, was murdered in the Tower, and his body brought by river to Chertsey. He was afterwards removed to Windsor by Henry VII, who tried to get him canonized, but was put off by the enormous expenses demanded by the Papal Court.

With the exception of the frequent visits of Henry VII and Henry VIII, who appear to have made a halfway house of the Abbey, on their journeys from Windsor to their palace at Sheen, no remarkable event in the history of the Abbey has been recorded from the date of Henry VI's funeral in 1471, till the time of the reformation in 1537, when, on the 6th of July in that year, Abbot John Corderoy, in conjunction with fourteen monks, surrendered the Monastery to the King, Henry VIII. At this dissolution the annual revenue of the Abbey was estimated at £659 15s. 8d. The King, as head of the Church, accepted the surrender, and in the deed it is set forth, that the King, for "the honour of God and the health of his soul," proposed to refound the dissolved Priory of Bisham, in Berkshire, and to establish there the Abbot and bretheren of Chertsey, and to endow them with all the manors and possessions late belonging to Bisham. The establishment at Bisham endured for a very short period, for within twelve months Abbot Corderoy was obliged to surrender his newly-formed Monastery to the Crown.

The superior of Chertsey Abbey was one of the Mitred Abbots, who were privileged to wear Episcopal ornaments; but it does not appear that he was one of the Lords in Parliament.

At the final suppression of Bisham Abbey, all the Monastic estates belonging to Chertsey reverted to the Crown.

The following extracts from vol. 558 "Expenses of Repairs, '&c., Oatlands, Henry VIII.," preserved in the Public Record Office, show that the King availed himself very shortly after their dissolution, of both Chertsey and Bisham Abbeys, in the erection of Oatlands Palace, and in planting its orchard:-

> "The Kyng's Maner of Otlonde. Ao. xxix. r. Henr. VIII. The Fyrste Boke for Otlonde Maner."
>
> "Itm payd to John Gravett of Charsey for land carryage of ij lods of appell trees, payre trees and chere trees from Charsey Abbey to Otlands at vjd the lode" (p. 163).
>
> "Also payd to Xpor Deconsoce, Mr. Bryklayere, for his costs and expenses, rydyng to Charsey Abbey and Byssam Abbey for provysyon of ston by the space of x dayes for hymself and hys horse at xijd. the day--xs. sol"- (p.335).

The site of Chertsey Abbey, previously held by Sir Anthony Browne, was granted to Sir William FitzWilliam, in the reign of Edward VI. In the time of James I, it again became Crown property and "the site, house, .and circuit" of the Abbey were granted by that Monarch to Dr. John Hammond, Physician to the King and Prince Henry. It descended to his son, Dr. Henry Hammond, who was one of the Chaplains of Charles I, and as such attended him in Carisbrooke Castle, when he was under the surveillance of Colonel Robert Hammond who was the doctor's nephew. Dr John Hammond died in 1660.

Aubrey, who published his "Antiquities of Surrey" about 1673, says:-

"Of this great Abbey scarce anything of the old building remains, except the outwalls about it. Out of the ruins is built a fair house, which is now in the possession of Sir Nicholas Carew, master of the buckhounds. The town lies very low, and the streets are all raised by the ruins of the Abbey."

The "fair house" was known afterwards as the Abbey House, and was taken down and all the materials sold and removed in the year 1810.

The best account we have of the site, since the destruction of the Abbey, is in a letter by Dr. Stukeley, written in 1752:-

"I went with eager steps to view the Abbey, or rather the site of the Abbey, for so total a dissolution I scarcely ever saw, so inveterate a rage against even the least appearance of it, as if they meant to defeat even the inherent sanctity of the ground. Of that noble and splended pile, which took up four acres of ground, and looked like a town, nothing remains; scarcely a little of the outer walls...

"The gardener carried me through a court on the right hand side of the house, where, at the entrance of the kitchen garden, stood the Church of the Abbey; I doubt not, splended enough. The west front and tower steeple were by the door and outward wall, looking towards the town and entrance to the Abbey. The east end reached up to an artificial mount, and all the terraces of the pleasure garden on the back-front of the house, are entirely made up of the sacred *rudera* and rubbish of continual devastations.

"Human bones of the abbots, monks, and great personages, who were buried in great numbers in the Church, were spread thick all over the garden, which takes up the whole of the Church and Cloisters, so that one may pick up handfuls of bits of bones at once, everywhere... Foundations of the religious buildings have been dug up, carved stones and slender pillers of sussex marble, monumental stones, effigies, crosses, inscriptions, everywhere; even beyond the terraces of the pleasure gardens.

"I left the ruins of this place, which had been consecrated to religion ever since the year 666, with a sigh for the loss of so much national magnificence and national history. Dreadful was the storm which spared not at least the churches, libraries, painted glass, monuments, manuscripts; that spared not a little out of the abundant spoil to support them for the public honour..."

In 1852 the site of the Abbey was purchased by Mr. Samuel Grumbridge, who, in searching for stone, accidently discovered a floor of concrete on which were the bulk of the tiles which form the subject of this book. I came to live in Chertsey in 1853, and made the acquaintance of Mr. Grumbridge. I caught sight of some tile fragments in a large heap of debris in his yard, and asked him their origin. I found that the designs were very superior to any I had seen before, and, as Mr. Grumbridge shared my enthusiasm, he had all the fragments picked out and cleaned. By arranging and collating these fragments, I succeeded in making out about thirty subjects more or less perfect.

Mr Herbert Minton and Sir Gilbert G. Scott inspected the tiles, and started a fund for further research. Subsequently, excavation work was undertaken headed by the Surrey Archaeological Society. During this work, many fresh fragments of the pavement, less worn and more perfect in design, were uncovered, and a stone coffin found in the Chapter House was nearly full of tiles.

I also inspected tiles which had previously come

from the site, at Little Kimble Church, Bucks. The Rector had them laid in the chancel in front of the altar rails, when the church was restored in 1872. The tiles there are illustrations of the romance poems, Sir Tristrem, and King Richard.

At Hales-Owen, near Birmingham, during an excavation made on the site of its Abbey in 1870, tiles more or less imperfect, bearing the designs of the historiated Chertsey tiles were discovered. Some of the pieces found at Hales-Owen enabled me to fill up some imperfect designs of tiles previously dug up at Chertsey. Among them is one representing Abbot Nicholas, identified from an inscription forming a border to the filling-in tiles, and thereby giving a clue to the date of manufacture of the pavement. The Abbot was living in the time of Henry III, and died in 1208. It was probably laid, therefore, in the beginning of the reign of Edward I. The designs - resembling those of the Chertsey pavement - on the Hales-Owen tiles refer only to incidents related in the romance poem of Sir Tristrem; and the filling-in tiles were of one shape only, and resembled those forming the square frames to the medallions at Chertsey. The design was also imitated, but the foliage was less conventional, the maple leaf apparently being represented. The pavement must therefore be considered of a later date than that of Chertsey (plate 35). For confirmation of the date assigned here to the tiles the reader is referred to the notes at the end of this section, on the subject of the armour represented on them.

It is probable that the more perfect tiles were removed at the time of the destruction of the Abbey. The mutilated condition of those remaining is thought by some to have been intentional, but it is more likely due to heavy stones falling, and the wheels of laden carts, during the demolition.

None of the medallions were found perfect, but

by finding repetition pieces bearing the same design, I was enabled to put together the designs as they are represented, without having to resort to conjecture.

The forms of the tiles vary, and several of the patterns are formed of very small pieces, resembling mosaic work, others again are very large. Thus, the small circles only an inch and a half in diameter, were also made in halves and quarters. The medallions are about ten inches in diameter; the rectangular tiles vary in size from nine to two inches.

Of the general design of the pavement, we can form a very inadequate idea. The most conspicuous portion was evidently the medallions, made as a single tile, in four quarters, and sometimes in nine parts, surrounded by a border which was homogeneous with the tiles, four forming a square frame (plates 35 and 39).

The border consisted of grotesques or inscriptions in French and Latin - the lettering being of the ordinary Lombardic character - descriptive of the subject enclosed, the portion of the tile adjoining the border being covered with conventional foliage. At Hales-Owen these were the only kind of frame tiles found; but at Chertsey, tiles of a totally different shape were also used to frame the medallions. One design was considered, from it band-like treatment, to have been copied from embriodery. It is similar in details to that on the mitre of Thomas a Becket, preserved at Sens Cathedral (fig. 2, plate 37).

The bands between these filling-in tiles and the medallions were formed of short tiles (twelve being required to encircle one medallion), bearing designs resembling a coronet and geometrical figures, and also inscriptions in Latin. The letters, all capitals, being more Roman in form than those previously mentioned, and what are called pearl letters, from having small circles or imitation of pearls attached to the centres of the upper and lower curves of the rounded ones. The angles of the filling-in pieces are occupied by circular tiles (fig. 3, plate 40) enriched by the busts of kings, queens, bishops, and grotesques, also patterns of almost classic simplicity; and the same may be observed of the small square tiles which occur at the ends of the filling-up pieces (fig. 4, plate 40) as well as of the borders which doubtless separated the pavement into longitudinal strips.

Besides these medallions with their ornamental framework, and the tiles previously mentioned, there are many others, rectangular, from eight to five inches in size, having the seasons, labours of the months, signs of the zodiac, grotesques and chimerical animals depicted on them.

Some tiles, five and a half inches square, are worth noticing, the pattern consisting of circles containing busts of kings, queens, &c., separated by a foliated design (fig. 3, plate 40). The same design was also made larger, stamped on a seven-inch tile (fig. 5, plate 40).

The pictorial designs on the medallions were also stamped on square tiles, an architectural ornament being added on each side (plates 11 and 29).

The lettering was shaped to fit the medallions and rectilinear tiles. A straight foliated border pattern was also utilised to form an outer border of a large circle.

Another series, forming the frontispiece of this work, consists of three figures, an archbishop in the act of benediction, holding a crozier in his left hand; a king, bearing a palm branch in his right hand; and a queen with a sceptre in her right hand, and a squirrel on the left.

Many tiles were found bearing inscriptions, but most are fragmentary. Plate 36 shows the only inscription I have been able to assemble: "Morgan e se gens, tourne en Engleterre." I also recognized the name of Tristrem frequently repeated, and "Rex Rica-rdus" in Roman pearl capital letters on the small border tiles. This determined me to read the mediaeval romances of "Richard Coeur de Lion" and "Sir Tristrem." Having carefully read them, I was at once convinced that the pavement illustrated the leading incidents of these poems.

The designs showing a mounted knight in chain armour and coroneted helmet, whose shield was ensigned with three leopards, and another knight, with a single lion on his shield, these being the armorial bearings respectively of King Richard and Sir Tristrem, enabled me to recognize scenes in which these personages are represented.

The first scene in which Tristrem appears is "playing at chess in a ship with a captain from Norway." The last is, "his corpse extended on a bier, a priest at either end reciting the Office for the Dead, or Dirge."

Having identified thirty-eight subjects, of which I had made drawings together with notes on the parts of the poem which I thought they represented, I sent them to M. Paulin Paris, who was at that time preparing the life of Sir Tristrem for publication. M. Paulin Paris wrote to me, saying that he thought I had interpreted the designs as well as possible from the material available. He also pointed out, that although the inscriptions to the Tristrem tiles are in French, they do not follow the French prose romance of Tristrem, but rather the British romance poem of Thomas of Erceldoune. For example, in the French romance, Tristrem was the son of Miliadus, and not of Roland Ris, and there is no mention of Morgan. M. Paulin Paris added the opinion that the texts which gave Roland Ris as Tristrem's father, seem to belong to older traditions than those in which his father is called Miliadus.

/text continued on p. 101,
after plates section.

ILLUSTRATIONS OF "SIR TRISTREM"

PLATE 1

Tristrem playing chess with a captain from Norway.

"Ther com a schip of Norway
  To Sir Rohandes hold,
With hawks white and grey,
  And panes fair y fold;
A chequer he fond bi a cheire
  He asked who wold play;
The mariner spac bonair---
  'Child, what wiltow lay?'
'Oyain a hawke of noble air,
  Tventi schillinges to say;
Whether so mates other fair,
  Bere hem bothe away.' "

The game of chess is supposed to have been invented in the East, but it was early known to the Northern people; and skill in that interesting game was one of the accomplishments of a Scandanavian hero. It is therefore fitting that a Norwegian mariner is introduced as the antagonist of Tristrem. Norwegian hawks were highy esteemed in England. Chess is frequently mentioned in ancient romance. In that of "King Richard" we read:---

"The messengers them hyed hard,
Till they came to King Richard.
They found King Richard at play,
At the chess in his galeye;
The Earl of Richmond with him play'd,
And Richard won all that he layd."

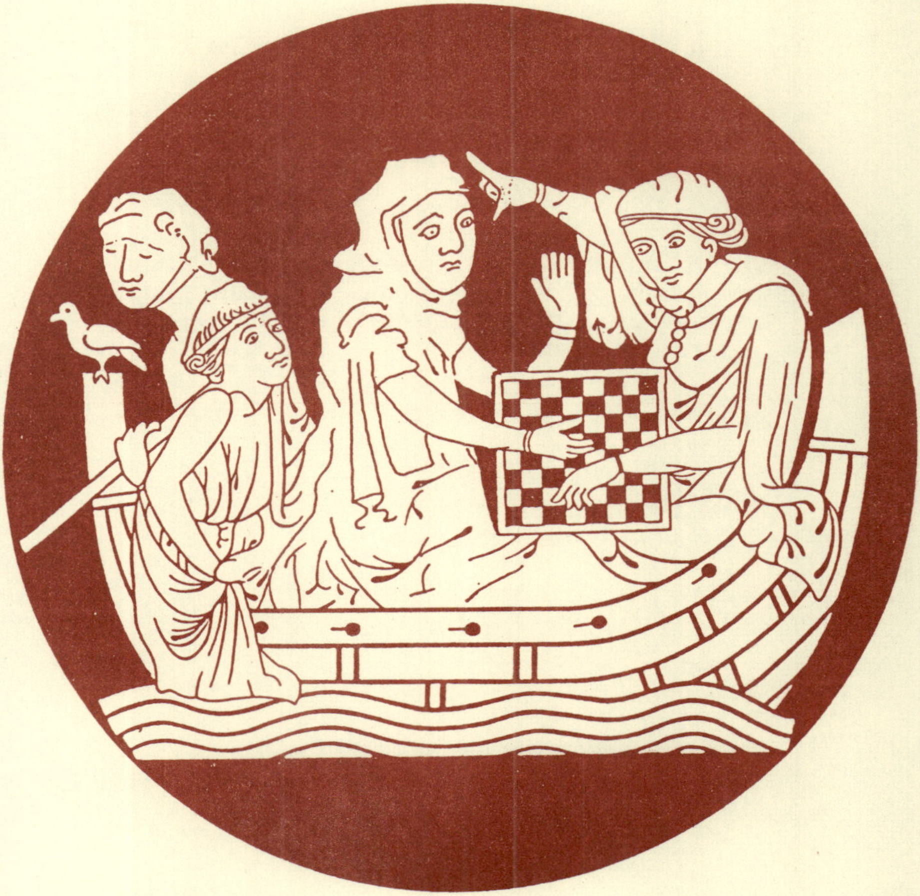

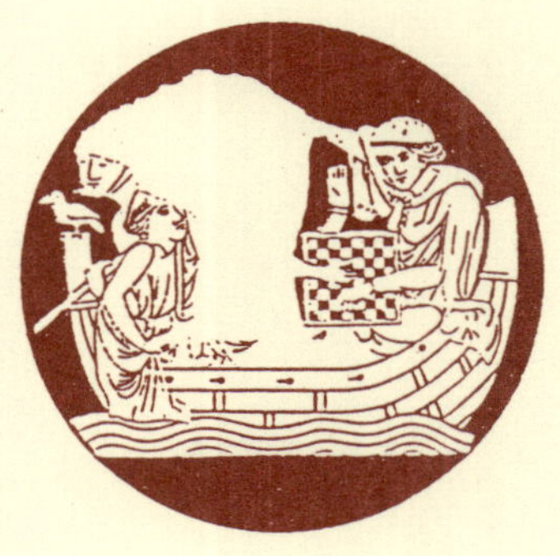

PLATE 2

Tristrem playing the harp before King Mark.

Tristrem having criticised the minstrel's playing, the harper retired in displeasure, saying:---

"Who better can lat se."

Tristrem immediately embraced the challenge, observing that he blamed the minstrel unjustly unless he himself could surpass him. After hearing him play

"The harpour gan to say,
'The ma'stri give y the
Ful sket:'
Bifor the kinges kne,
Tristrem is ca'd to set."

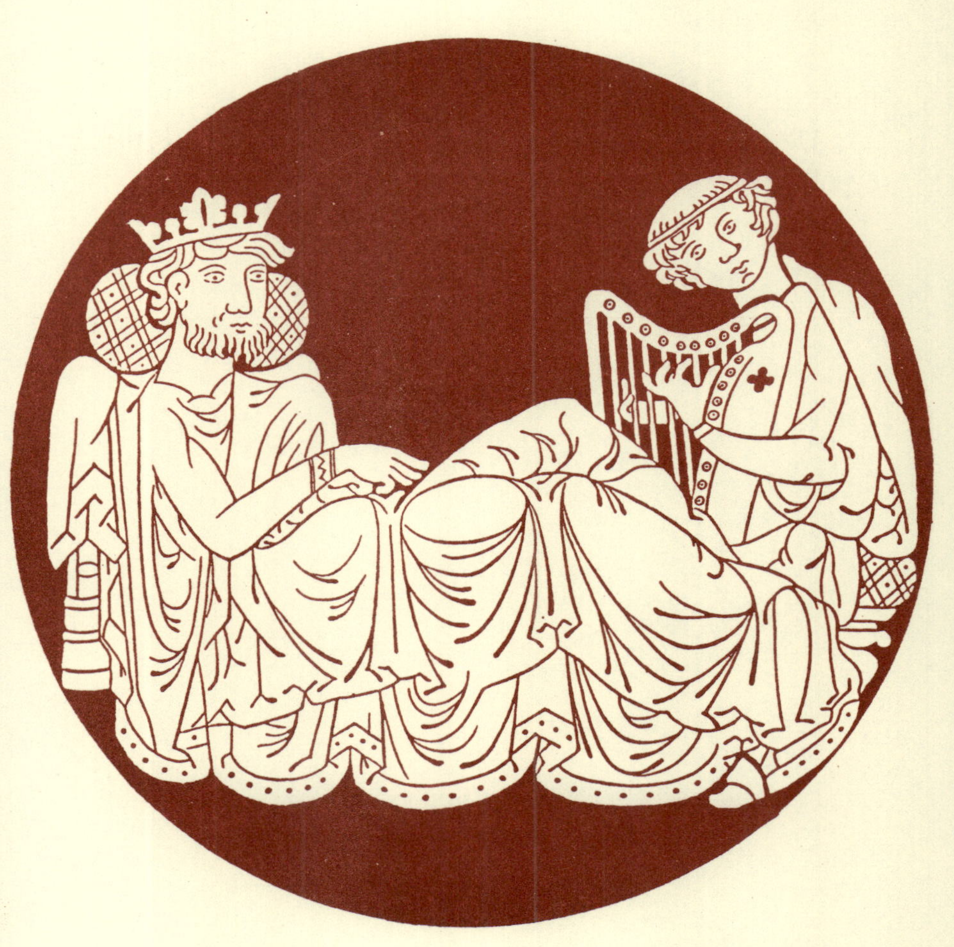

PLATE 3

Rohand is refused admittance to the castle of King Mark, on account of his mean and tattered garments.

"His robes riuen were."

He is represented holding a glove to show his nobility.

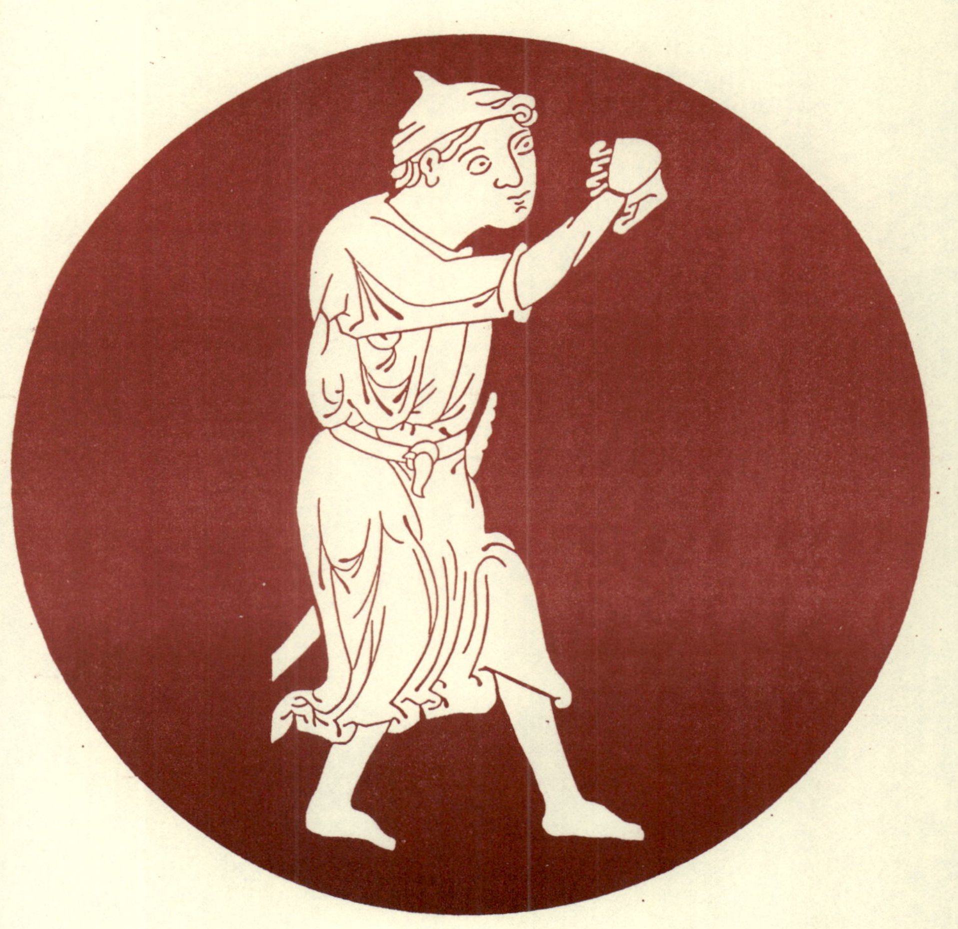

PLATE 4

The porter at King Mark's castle.

"The porter gan hym wite,
  And seyd, 'Cherl, go oway,
Other y schal the smite,
  What dostow here al day?' "

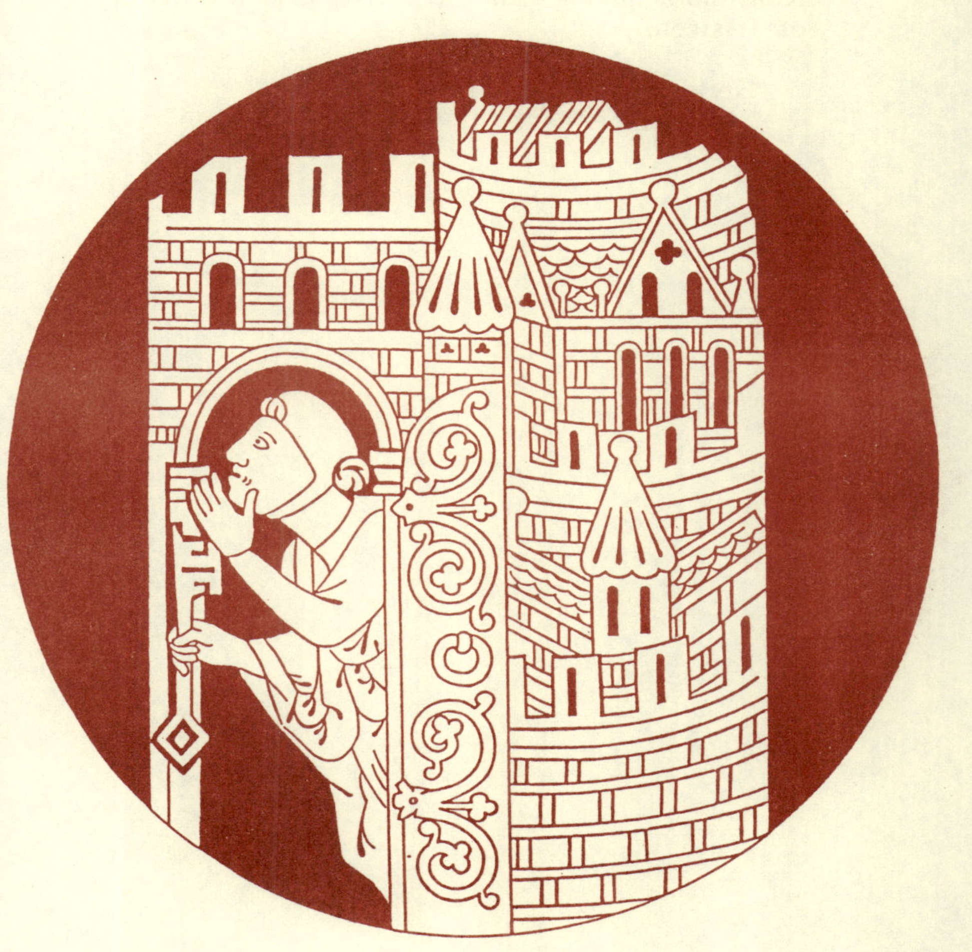

PLATE 5

King Mark having heard from Rohand the history of Tristrem.

> "He kissed Tristrem ful skete.
>   And for his nevou toke."

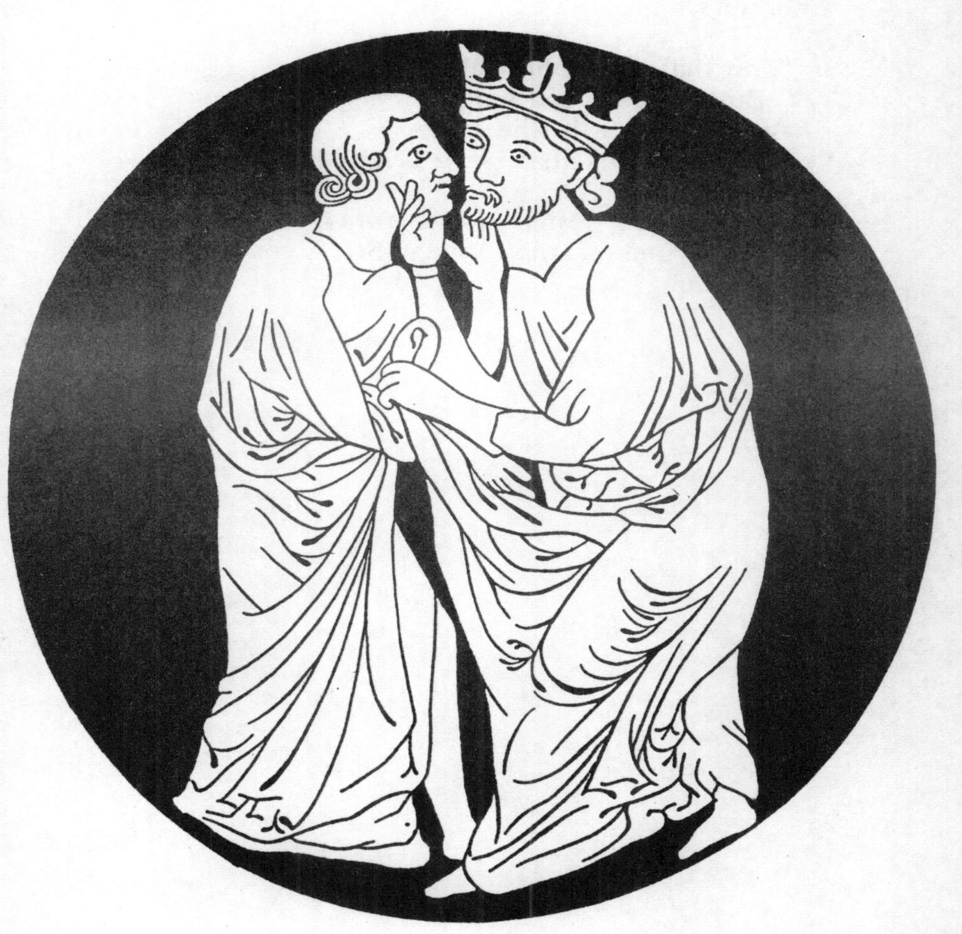

Plate 6

Tristrem congratulated and kissed by all the Courtiers.

"Tho thai kisten him alle,
  Bothe leuedi and knight,
And seraiunce in the halle,
  And maidens that were bright."

This imperfect design was drawn from fragments of tiles found at the Abbey, St. Ann's Hill, and Hales-Owen.

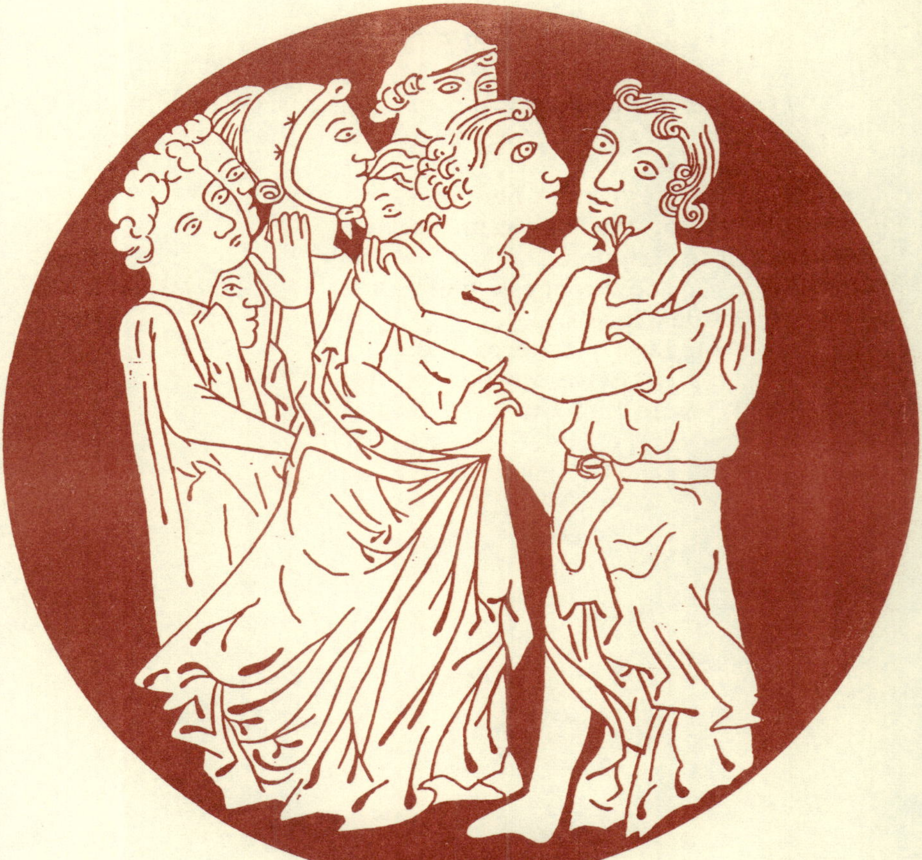

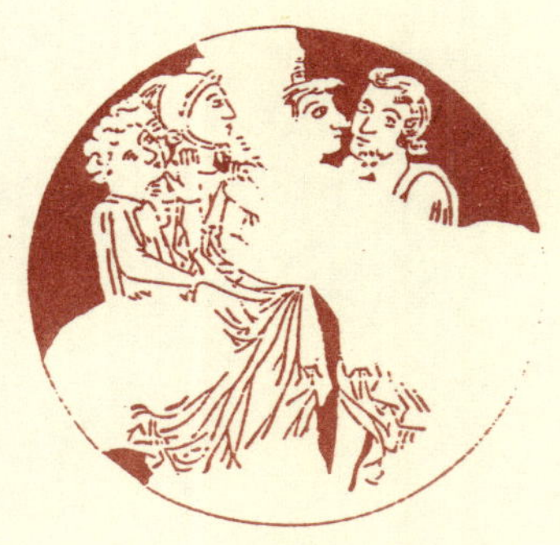

PLATE 7

Tristrem announces to the king his determination to go to Ermonie to avenge his father's death.

"Tristrem al in heighe,
  Bifor the king cam he;
'Into Ermonie,
  Sir, now longeth me;
Thider fare wil y,
  Mi leue y take of the;
To fight with Morgan in hy,
  To sle him other he me.' "

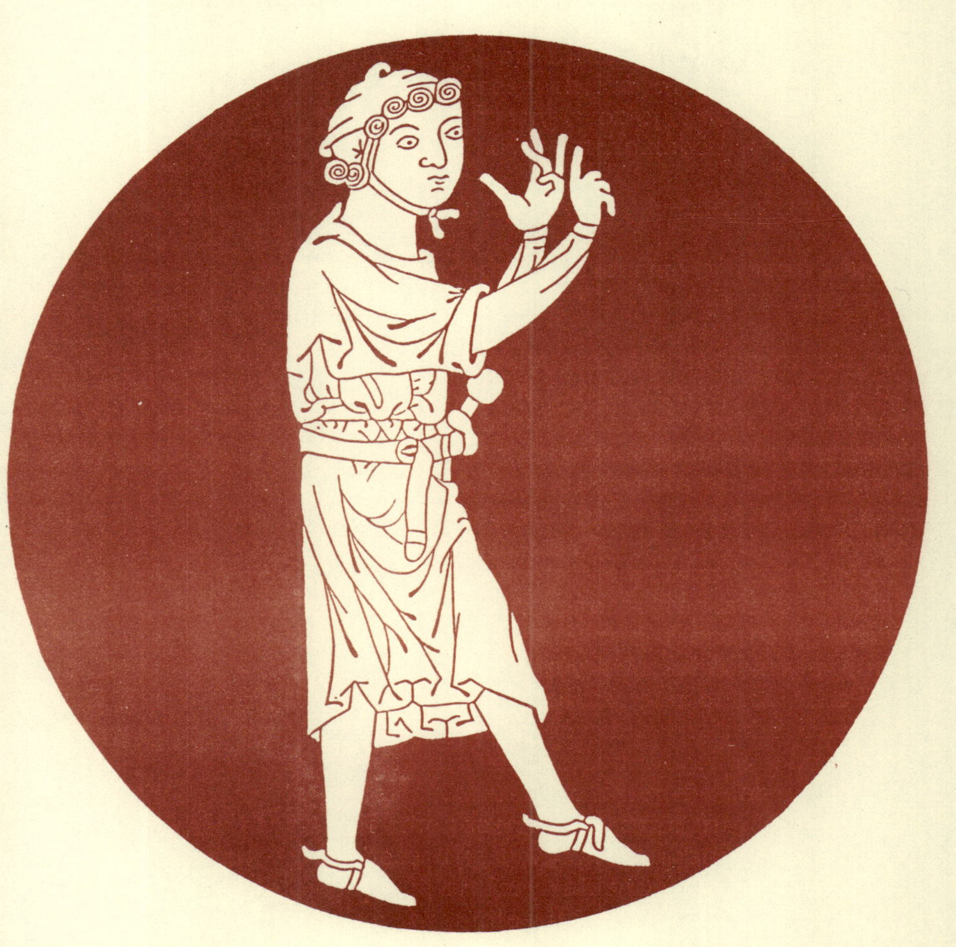

PLATE 8

King Mark dissuading Tristrem from going to Ermonie, but he at length gives his consent, and bestows upon him the honour of knighthood.

"To help Tristrem for thi,
He made knight with his hond."

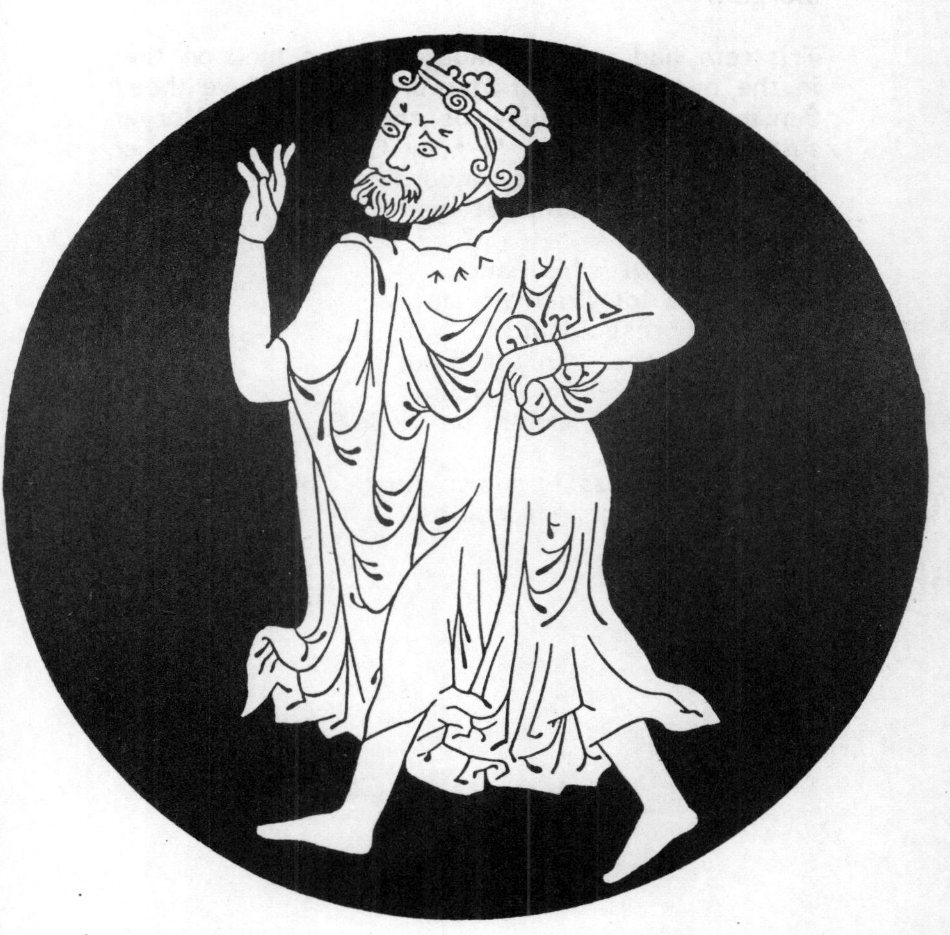

PLATE 9

Tristrem (disguised) in angry parley with Duke Morgan.

Tristrem had said to Morgan, "God look on thee in the measure that I love or ought to love thee." Sensing the ambiguity of the situation, Morgan suits his reply to it, "I pray God to requite thee in blessings or curses, according to your meaning." After mutual recriminations

"Morgan with his hand,
  With a lof Tristrem smot.
On his brest adoun,
  Of his nose ran the blod;
Tristrem swerd was boun,
  And ner the Douke he stode."

The duke's dress is shown lined with vair (a kind of fur), only worn by nobles.

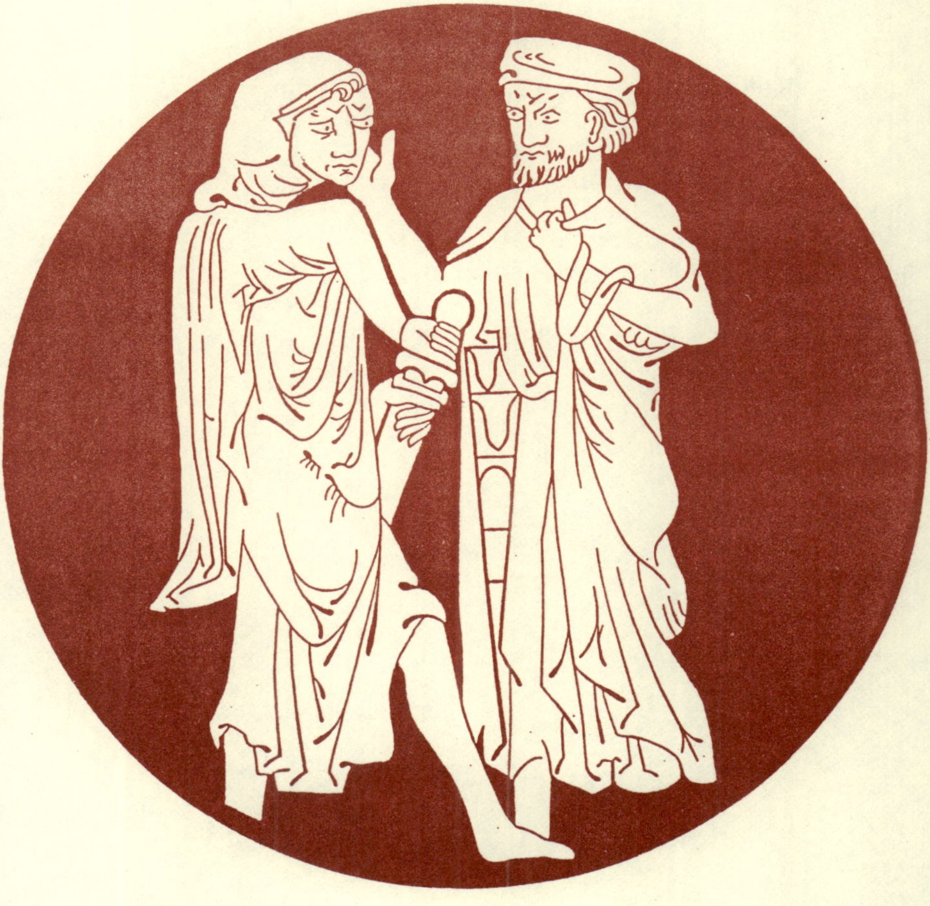

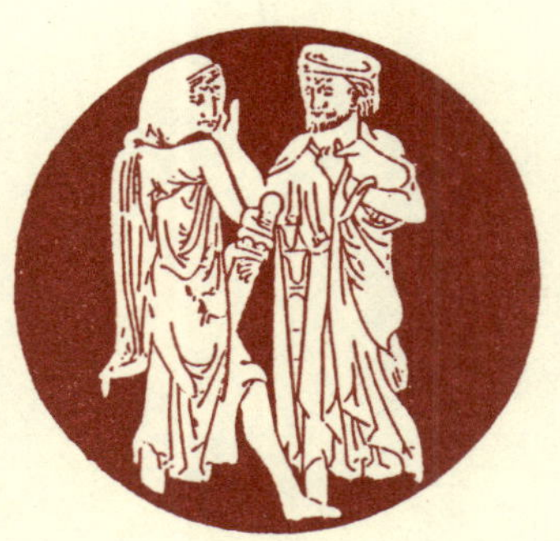

PLATE 10

Rohand made Liege Lord of Ermonie.

"Rohand he yaf the wand,*
  And bad him sitt him bi,
   That fre;
'Rohand lord make y,
  To held this lond of me.'"

*The wand or symbol of power.

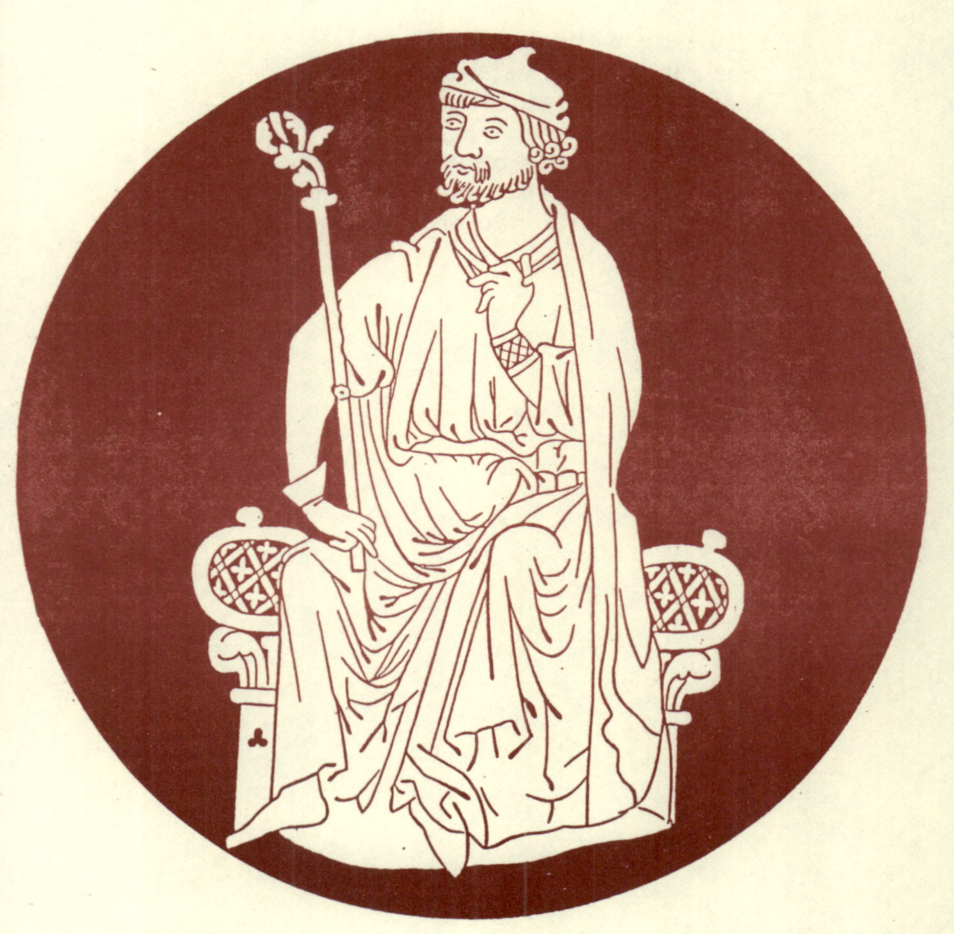

PLATE 11

Children brought as tribute to King of Ireland.

"Mani man wepen sare,
  For ransoun to Yeland,
Three hundred barnes fre."

The fragment of tile above the medallion is preserved in the British Museum, and shows that this design was stamped on both square and round tiles.

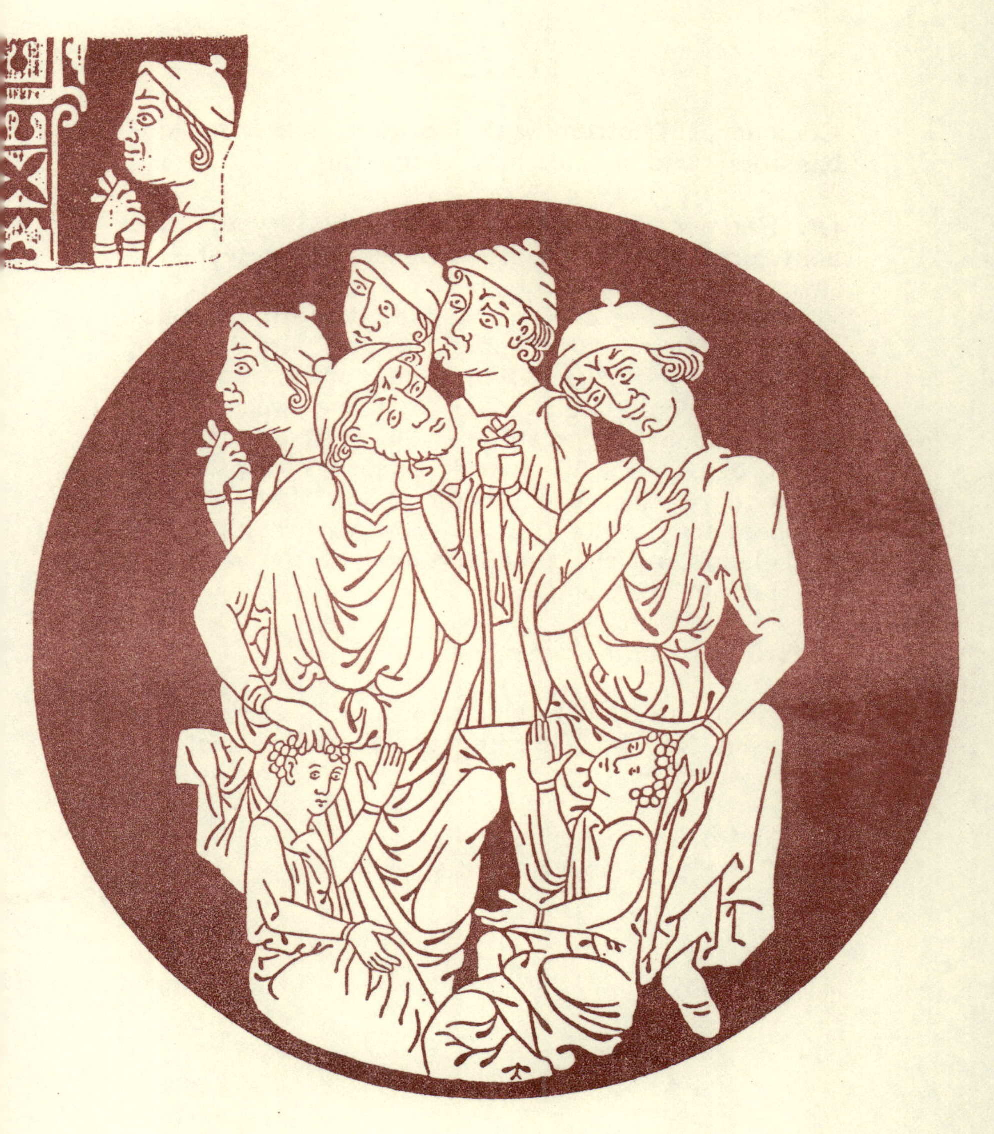

PLATE 12

Combat of Tristrem with Moraunt, the Irish Ambassador, who wounds him in the thigh.

Dr. Hanmer informs us that the history of Moraunt, preserved in the Book of Houth, states:---

> "Marke, King of Cornewayle, denieth the tribute, offereth the combate, and Sir Tristrem undertaketh it for him. The combatants meet and fiercely fight. The battaille was a long time doubtfull; in the end Sir Tristrem gave Sir Morogh, with his sword, a sòre blow, that a piece of the edge stucke in his skull, whereupon the combat ended. Moraunt returned to Ireland, and shortly after died of the wound." (Hanmer's Chronicle, 1633.)

> "He smot him in the lyoun."

This is an allusion to the armorical bearing of Sir Tristrem, which, according to all authorities, was a lion rampant.

> "And in the haunche right,
> Tristrem was wounded sare."

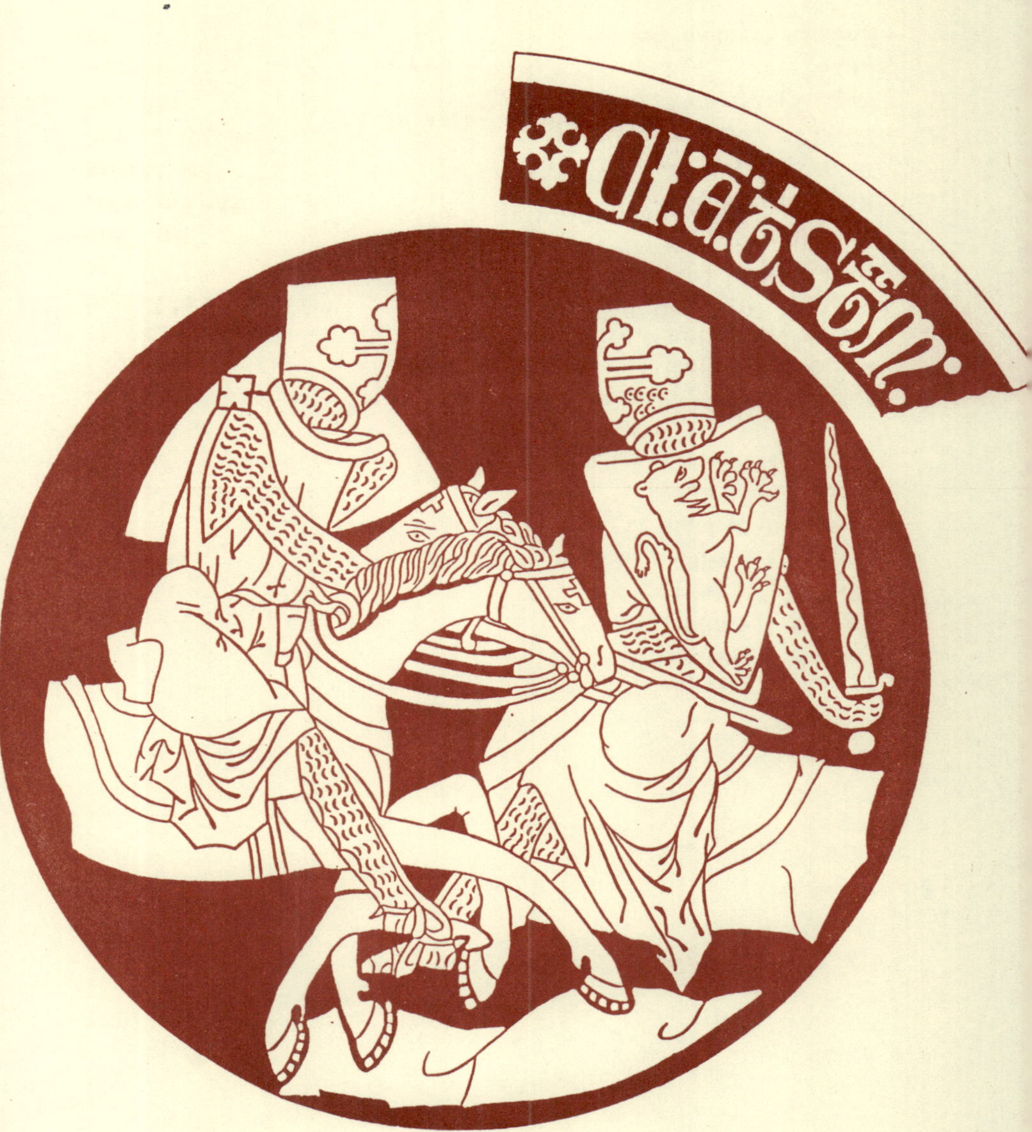

PLATE 13

Continuation of the combat of Tristrem with Moraunt.

"Tristrem smot with mayn,
  His swerd brak in the fight,
And in Morauntes brain,
  Bileued a pece bright." .

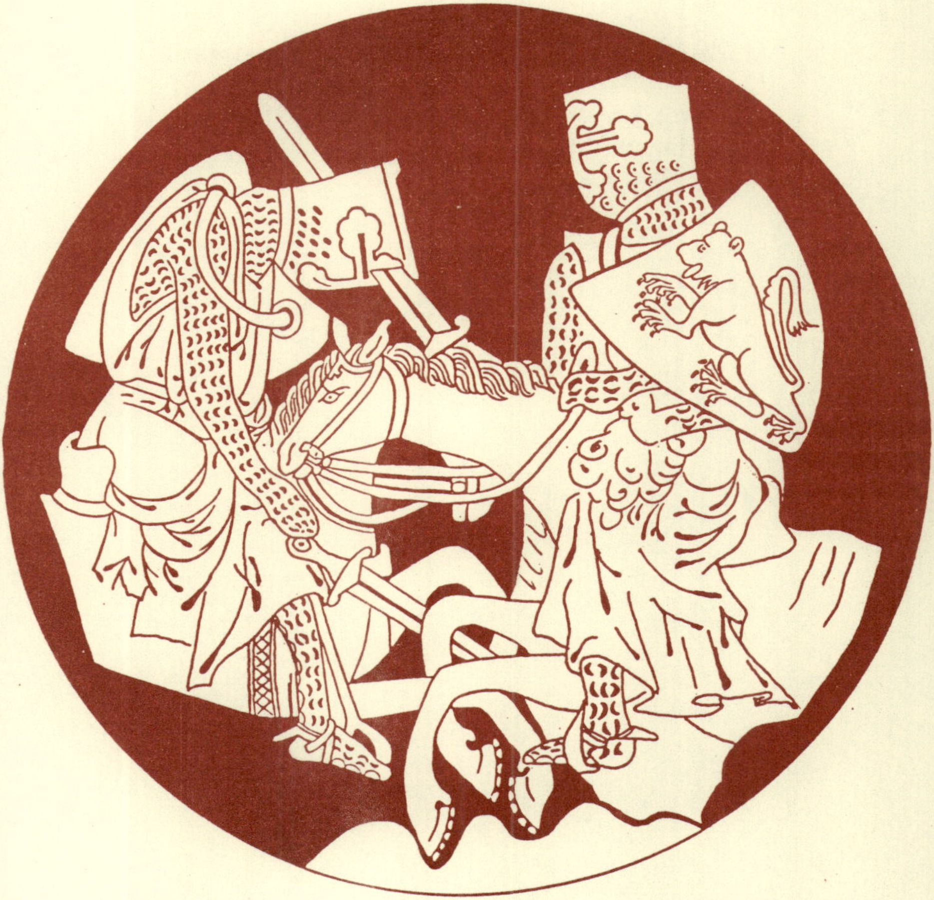

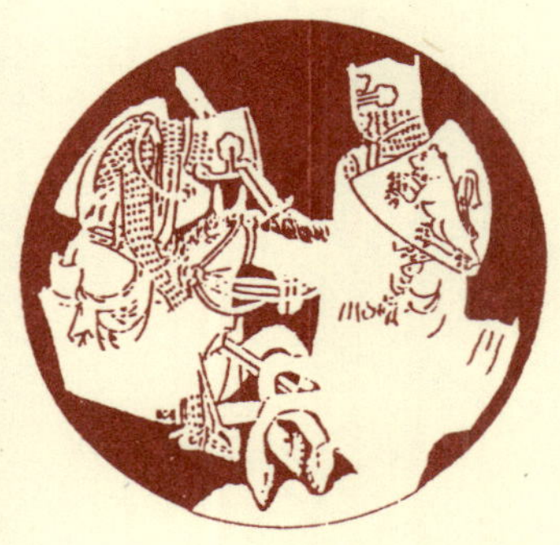

PLATE 14

Moraunt carried off for dead by attendants.

"With sorwe, thai drough, that tide,
Moraunt to the se,
And care."

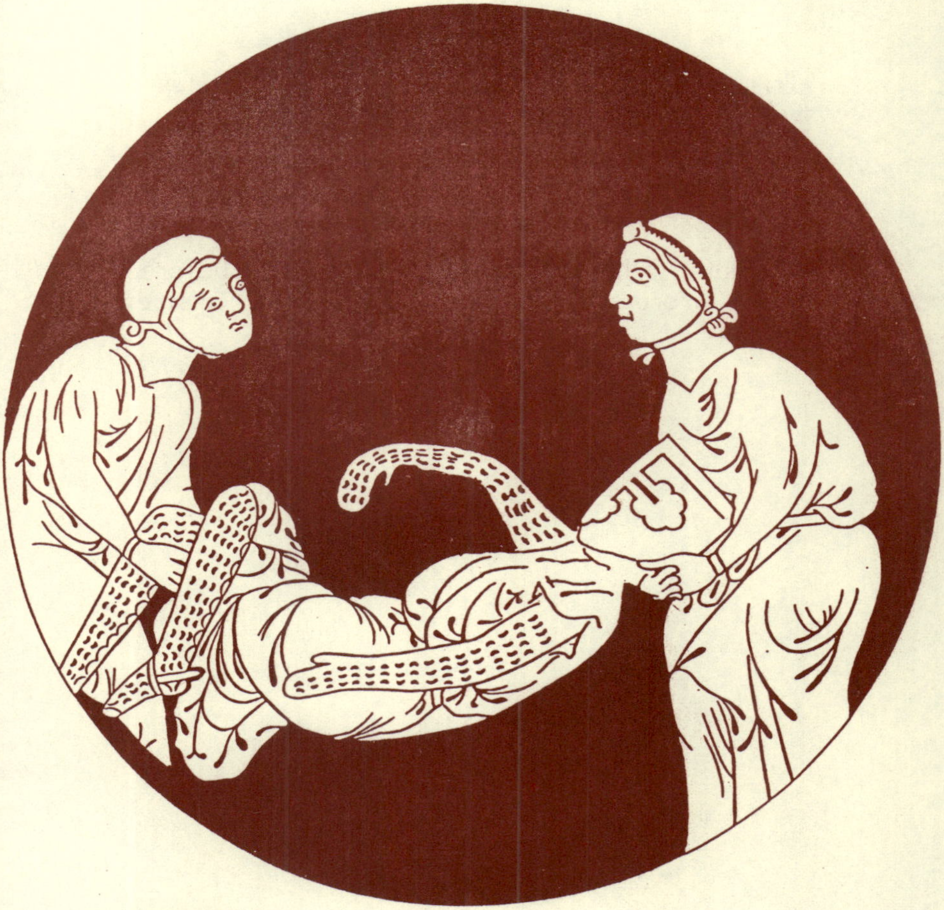

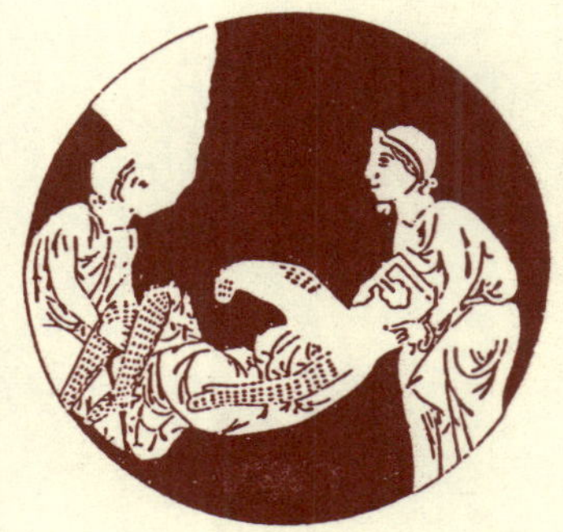

PLATE 15

Tristrem confined to his bed by a gangrenous wound, is visited by King Mark.

> "No man might bi him stand,
> For stinking of his wounde."

The king is holding part of his garment before his nose, in order to avoid the smell from Tristrem's wound.

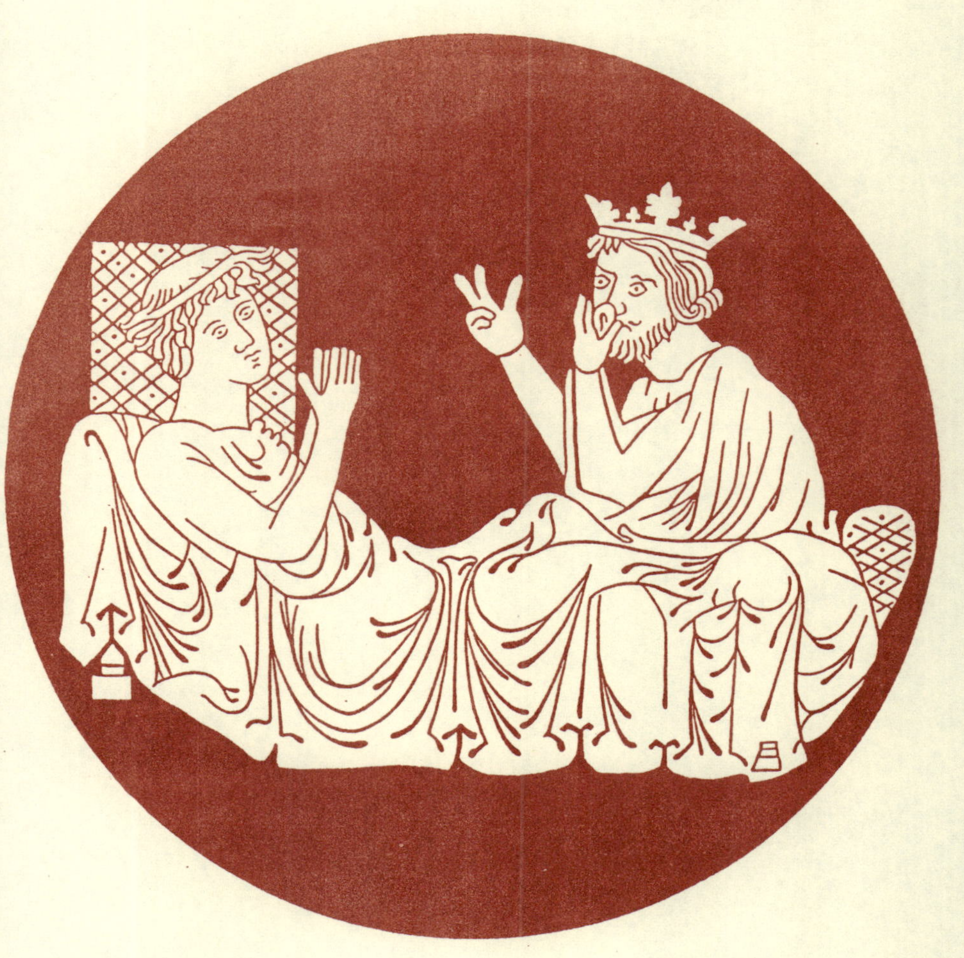

PLATE 16

The Queen of Ireland visits Tristrem in his ship.

"She sent him a plaster kene
  To cast the stink oway.

"Amorwe, when it was day,
  The leuedi of heighe priis,
Com ther Tristrem lay;
  And asked what he is?"

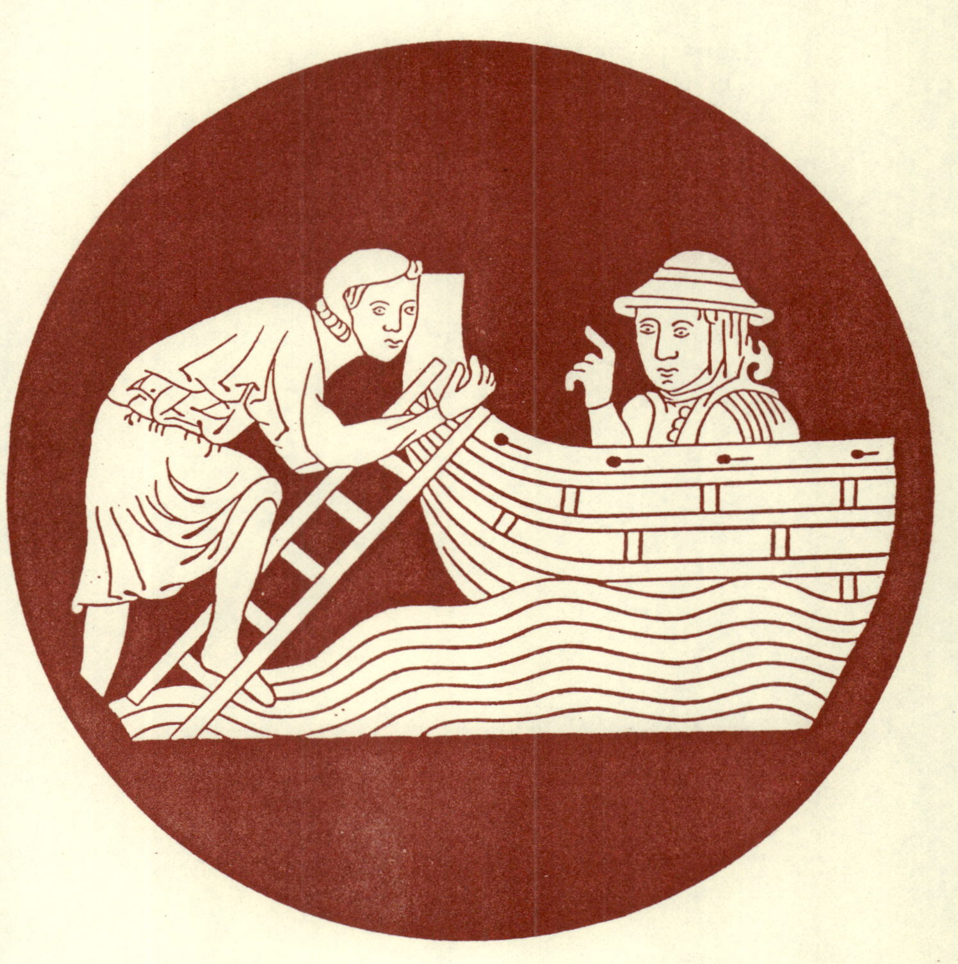

PLATE 17

Tristrem attacking the dragon.

"Asaut to that dragoun,
  Tristrem toke that tide,
As a lothely lioun,
  That bataile wald abide:
With a spere feloun,
  He smot him in the side."

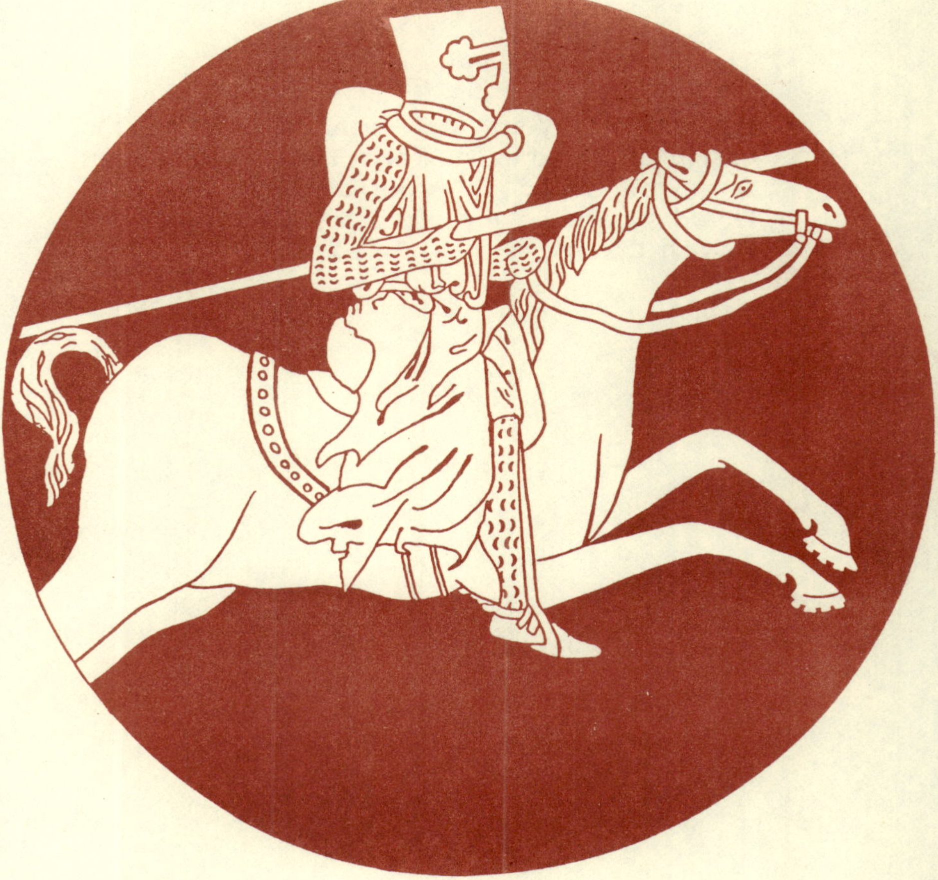

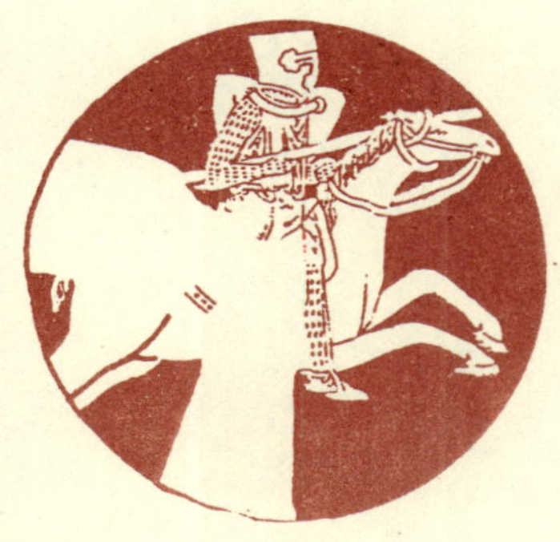

PLATE 18

The dragon of Ireland.

I have not myself met with any part of the design of the dragon. This plate is taken from fragments found at Hales-Owen by Mr. J. R. Holliday, who gave me a tracing, and identified it with this incident in the poem.

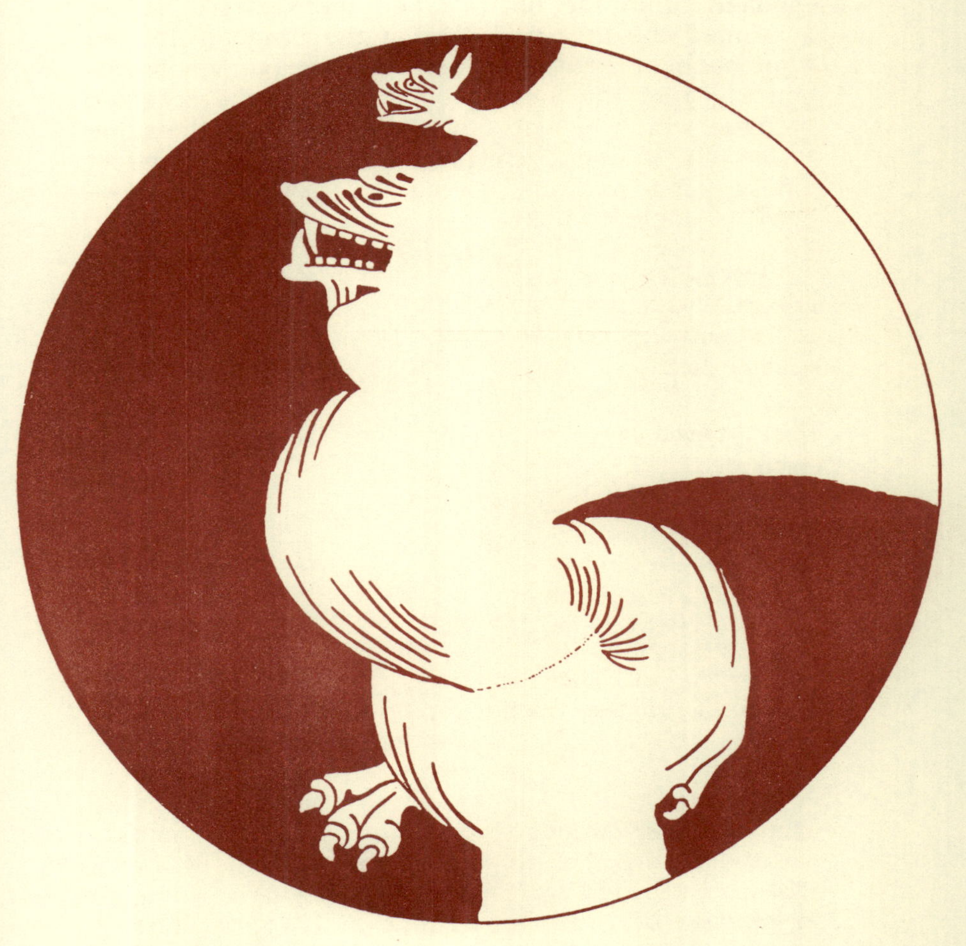

PLATE 19

The legal duel or wager of battle.

This interesting design, representing trial by combat, I suppose was introduced among the incidents of the life of Sir Tristrem because the subject is spoken of in the poem, when the steward having assumed the merit of slaying the dragon, claimed the hand of Princess Ysonde. Tristrem vindicates his right to the victory by producing the dragon's tongue which he had cut out, offering at the same time his ship and cargo in pledge that he would make good his story upon the person of the steward in single combat.

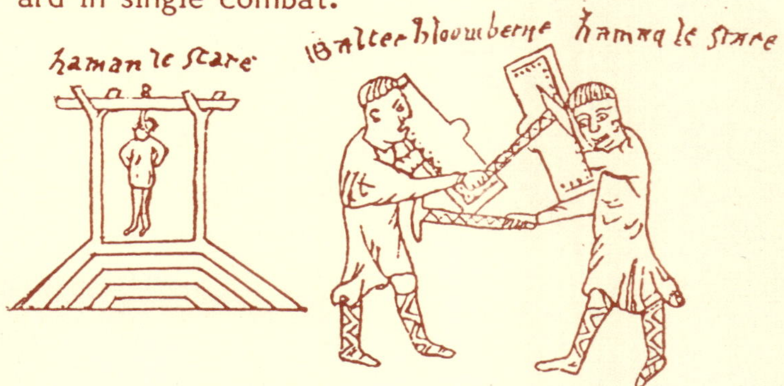

The above drawings are traced from one of the "Miscellaneous Rolls" in the Tower, of the time of Henry III. The document is noticed in Madox's "History of the Exchequer." He describes the incident as "a pretty remarkable case of a duell that was fought in the reign of Henry III... A duel was struck, and Hamon being vanquished in the combat, was adjudged to be hanged." The combatants are armed with a quadrangular shield and a "baston" headed with a double beak. According to a statute of Philip of France in 1215, the batons should not exceed three feet in length. Cropped hair and bare heads conform to another ordinance of the Camp-fight. The combattants shown on the tile are both armed with quadrangular shield and a baston headed with a double beak, and are bare-headed, with cropped hair, in conformity with the ordinance.

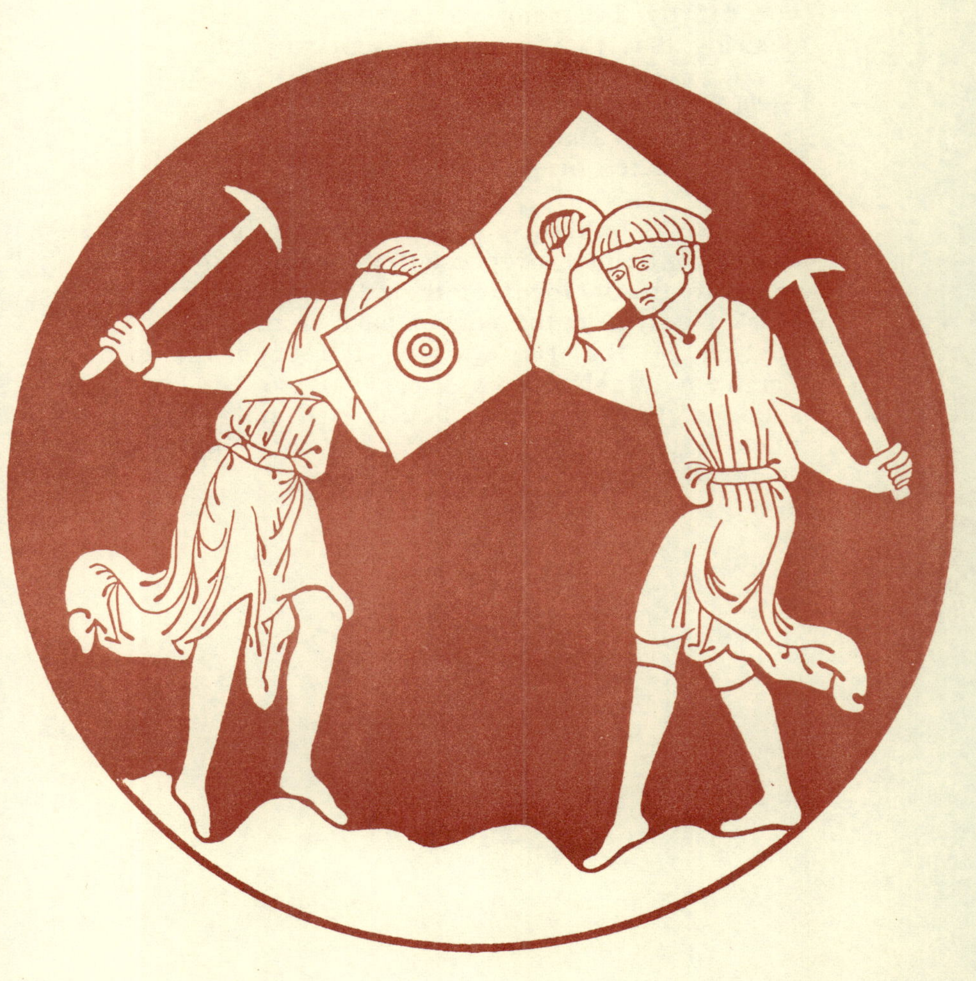

PLATE 20

Princess Ysonde showing the tongue of the dragon, cut off by Tristrem, to the King of Ireland, and desiring that the steward be sent to prison.

> "To bring
> To prisoun that other knight,
> The maiden biseketh the king."

Tristrem is holding a glove to denote his nobility. The two palmers represented behind him would refer to the incident of their leading him to King Mark's castle in the earlier part of the poem. The portion of the tile showing the upper parts of Tristrem and Isonde was previous to 1875 to be seen in the chancel of Little Kimble Church, Bucks. It was not re-laid when the church was restored.

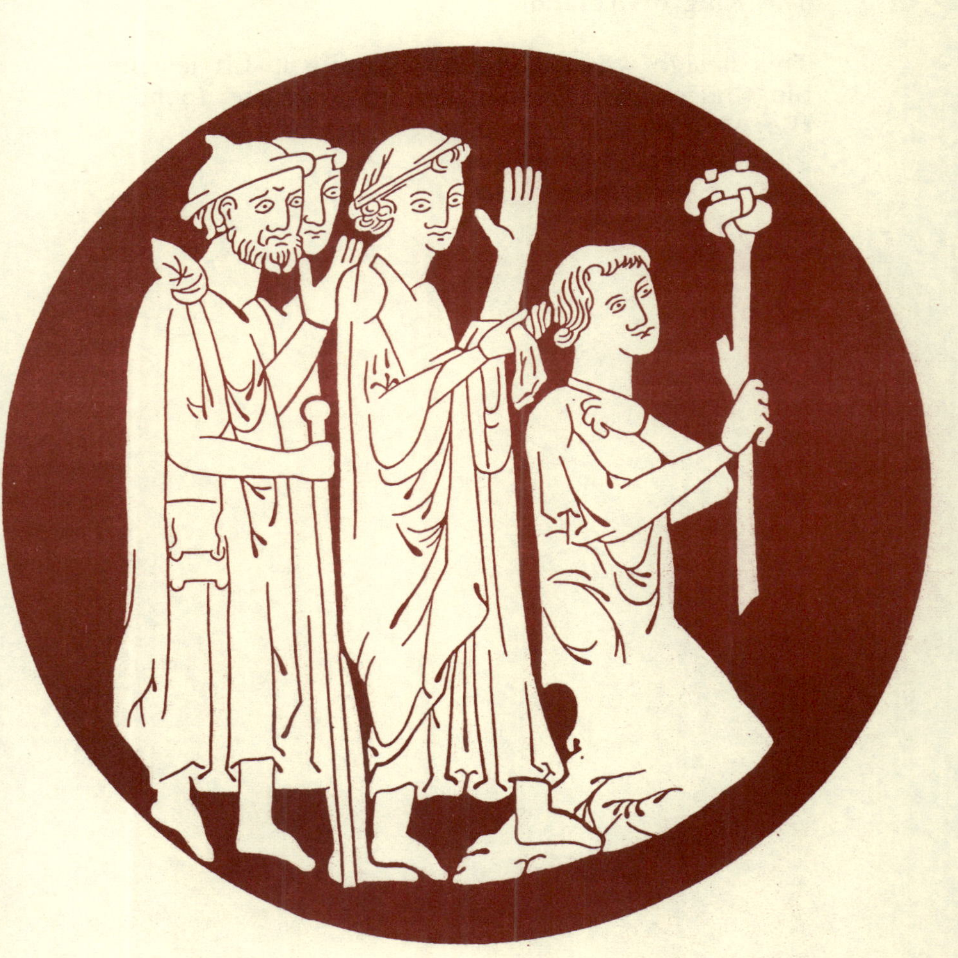

PLATE 21

The King of Ireland.

This design was copied from a tile in Little Kimble Church, being more perfect than any found at the Abbey.

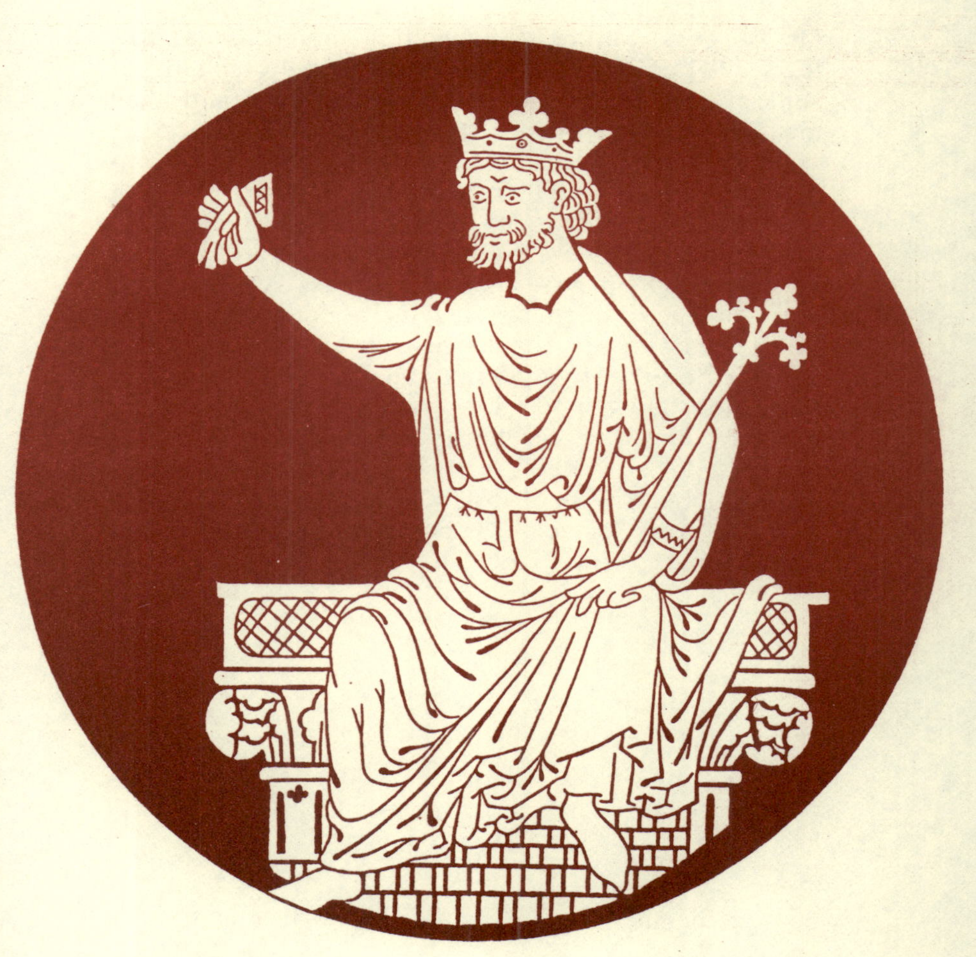

PLATE 22

Tristrem hunting wild beasts in the forest, with his greyhound named Houdain.

Mr Burgess commented on this medallion as follows: "Whoever may have been the original designer of this pavement he most certainly had classical models before his eyes... Several circumstances tend to make us suspect that the composition was copied from some antique original, perhaps a painting, but more likely a tessellated pavement... If we may believe the works left us by the Middle Ages, the poorest always had their legs covered, because it was a condition of the climate that they should be so. Another noticable point is the horse's hoofs, which in this instance have no shoes, while in the other medallions the nails of the horses' hoofs are exceedingly prominent... The want of stirrups is another proof of the antique origin of this Chertsey tile... Perhaps it is a copy of one of a series by some great Greek artist, now lost."

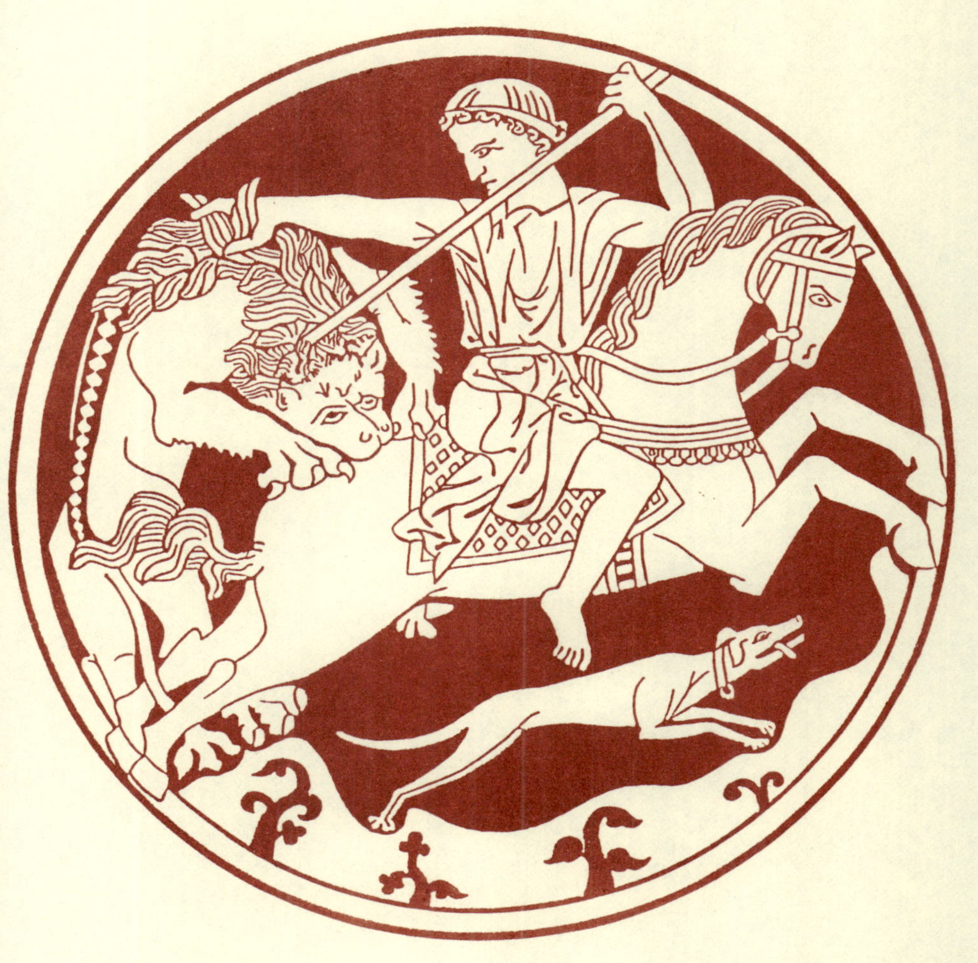

PLATE 23

Tristrem hunting with his bow.

Compare with plate 22.

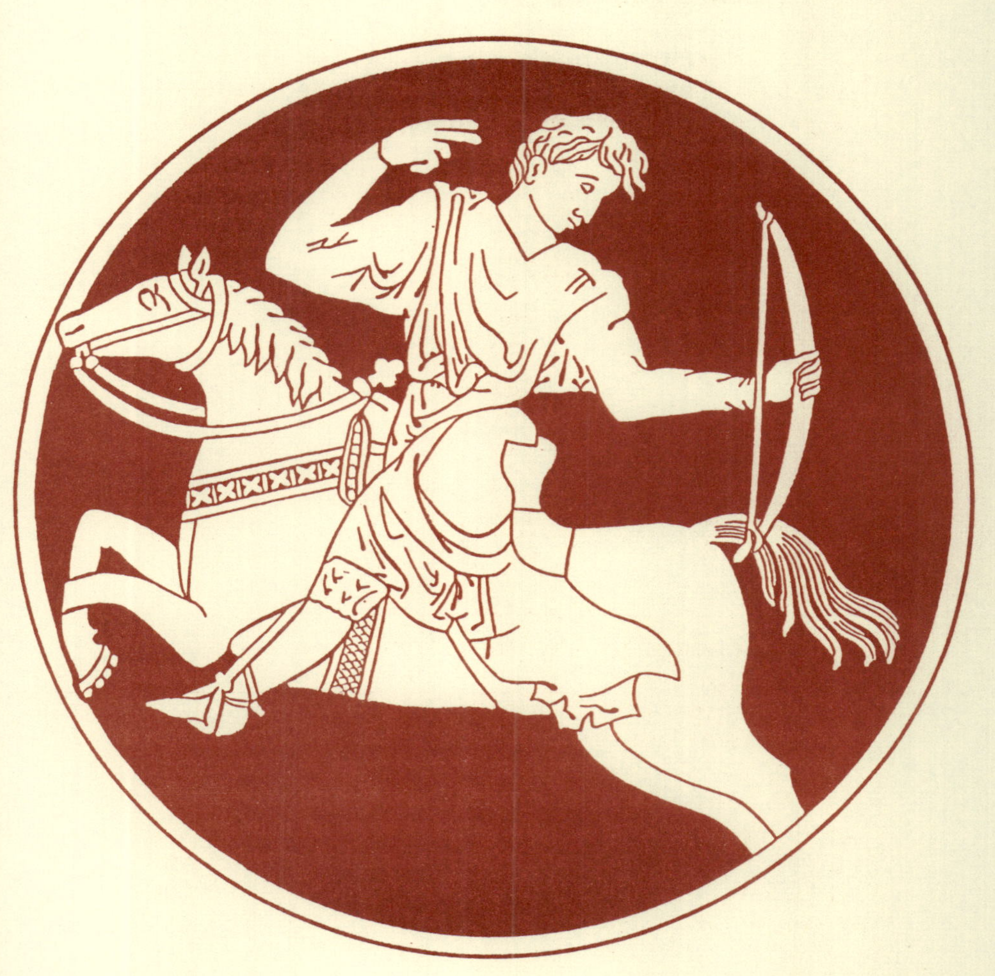

PLATE 24

Ysonde in a boat singing the songs of Tristrem.

"Tristrem made song,
  That song Ysonde the sleighe,
And harped euer among."

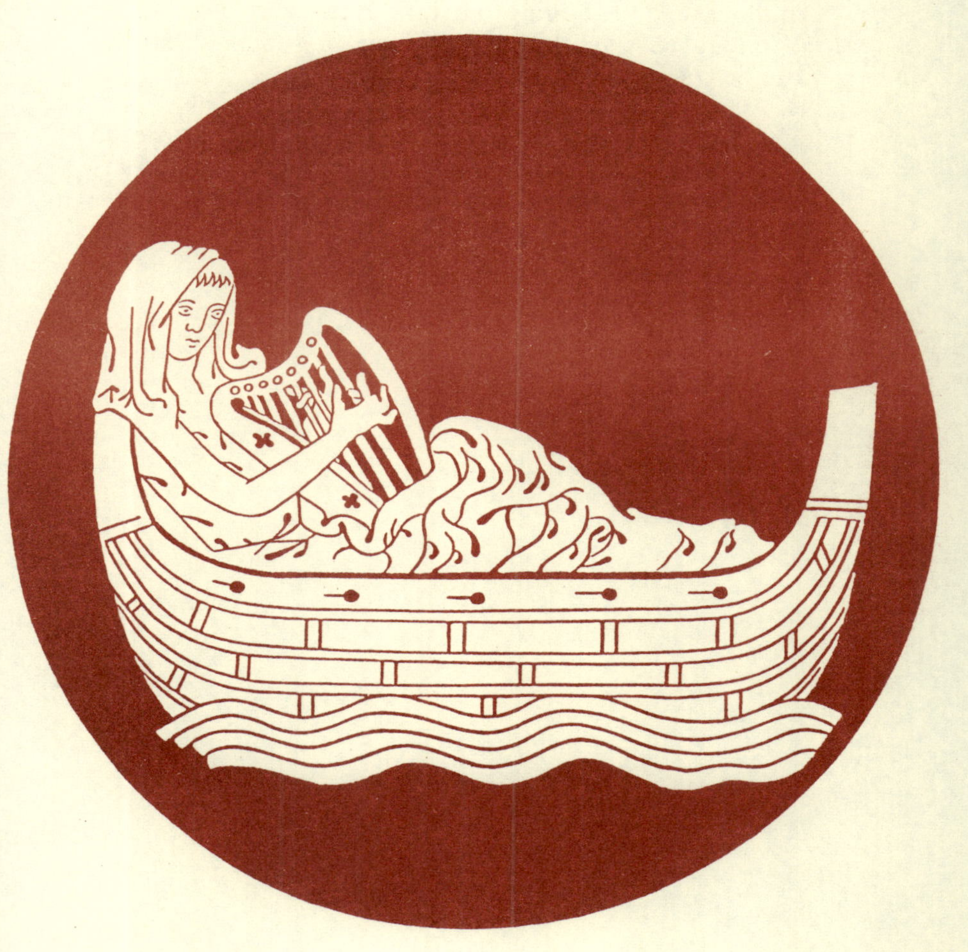

PLATE 25

Tristrem disguises himself as a court fool, feigns madness, and having obtained an interview with Ysonde, reveals himself by singing songs he had taught her.

This interesting design which tells its own tale so well, was only found in large fragments at Chertsey, but fortunately the whole of it was discovered at Hales-Owen.

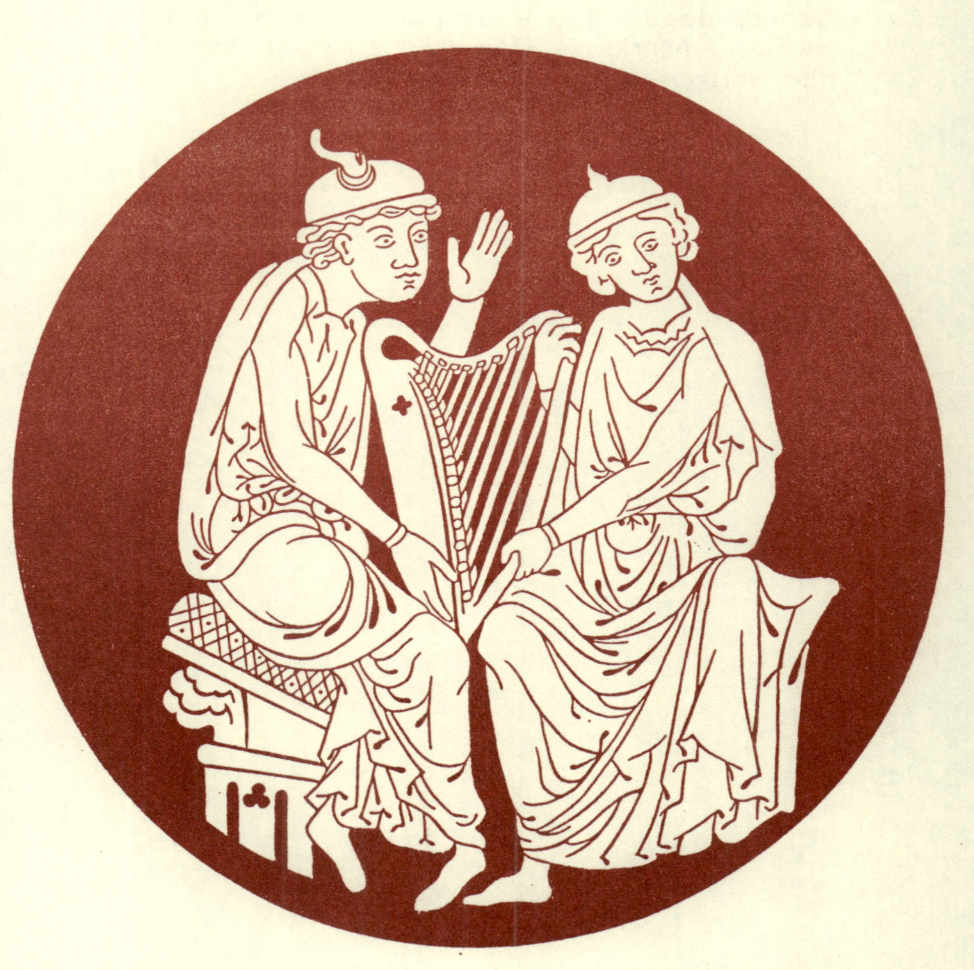

PLATE 26

Ysonde disguised as a man, accompanied by Brengwain, embarks in Ganhardin's vessel displaying the white sail.

> "Sche schope hir as a man,
> With Ganhardin to fare."

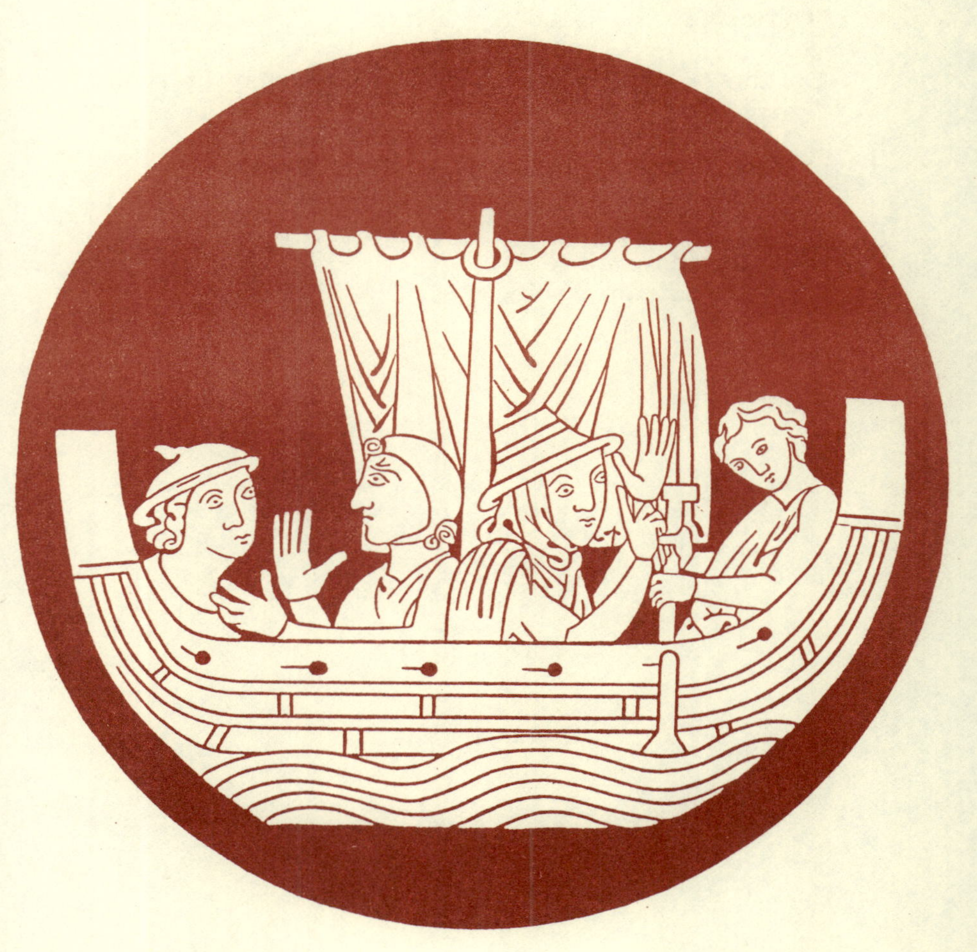

PLATE 27

Tristrem laid out. The priests are reciting the "Office for the Dead" or "Dirge."

On the book of the left hand figure may be read "Dirige Dne."

"The bellies con thai ring,
  And masses con thai seye,
    For dole;
  Prestes praised aye,
For Tristram's sole."

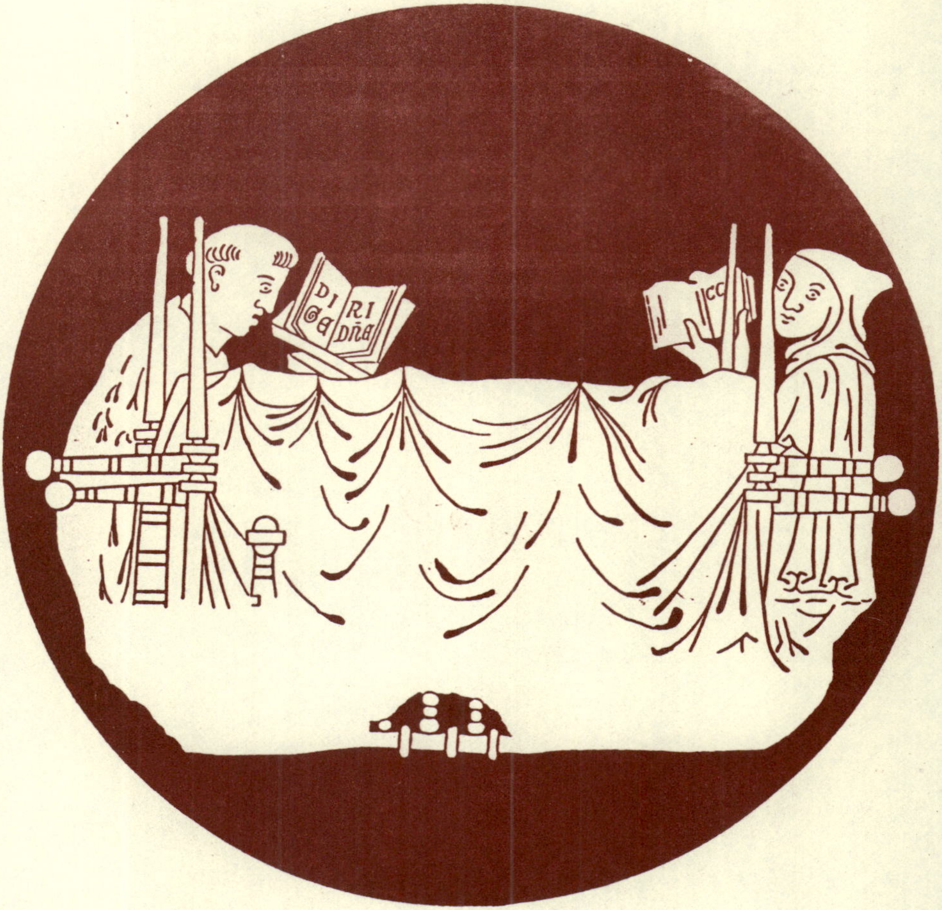

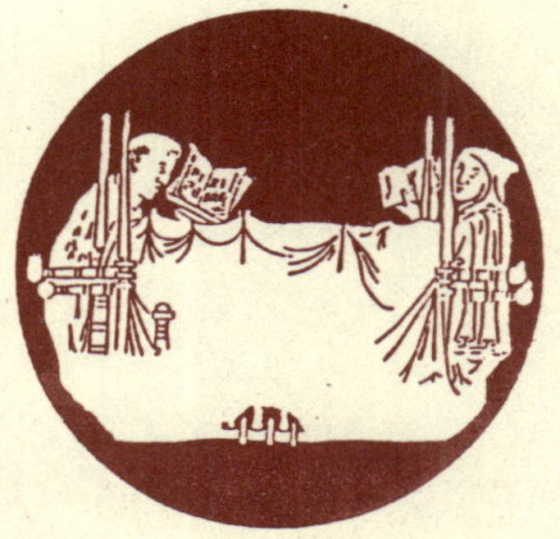

PLATE 28

King Richard's combat with the lion.

"The lyon wolde have hym al to-rent,
Kyng Rychard thenne besyde he glent,
Upon the brest the lyoun he spurnyd,
That al aboute the lyoun turnyd."

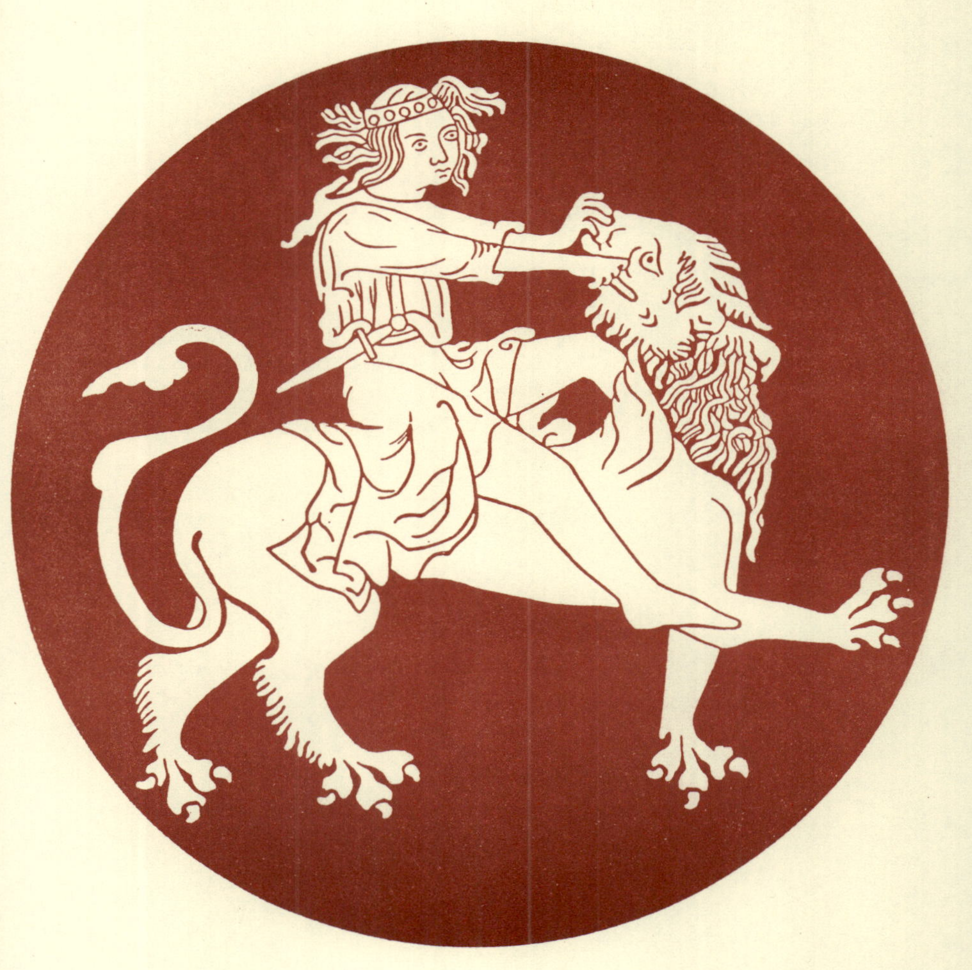

PLATE 29

A Saracen killed by a knight.

"An old knyght was, with Rychard bydis,
To the styward he spak, pryvy lyche:
'Our lord kyng sore is seke, I wis,
Afftyr pork he alongyd is,
Take a Sarezene yonge and fat,
In haste that the theff be slayn,
Openyd, and hys hyde off flayn,
And soden ful hastely,"

The way in which the hand could be withdrawn at pleasure from the hawberk, by an opening in the palm, is well shown, one hand of the knight being bare, the sleeve hanging loose.

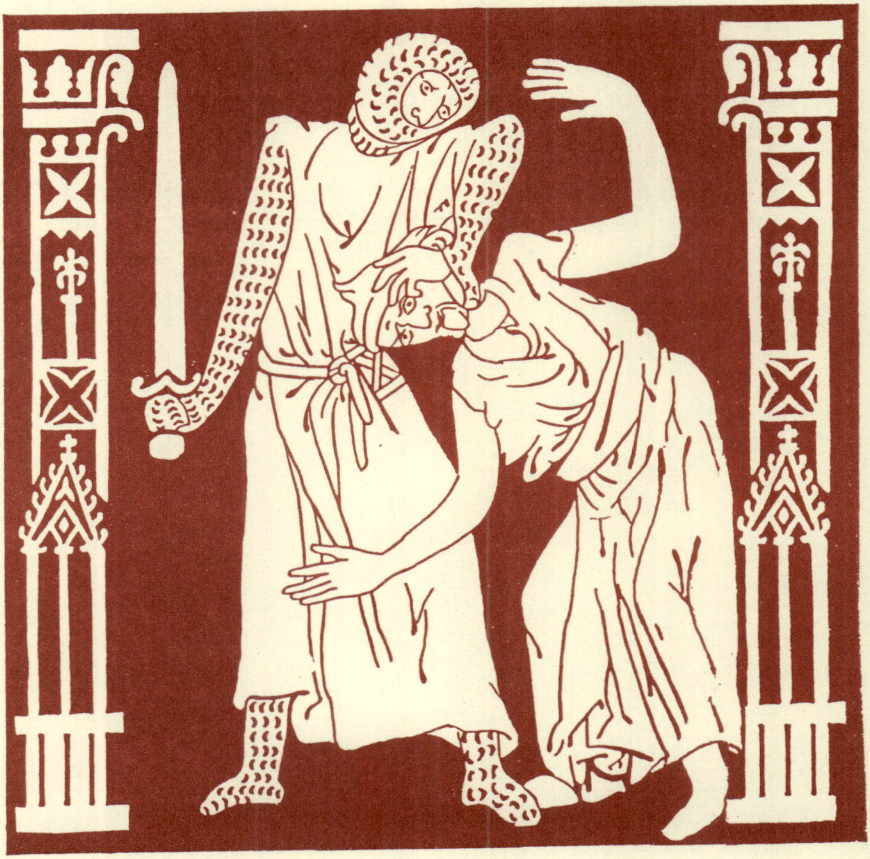

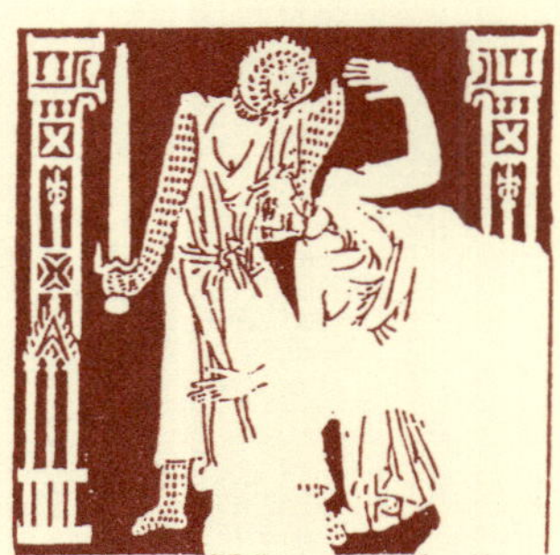

PLATE 30

King Richard in single combat with the Sultan Saladin.

King Richard is identified by his shield, ensigned with three leopards, and by the coronet on his helm.

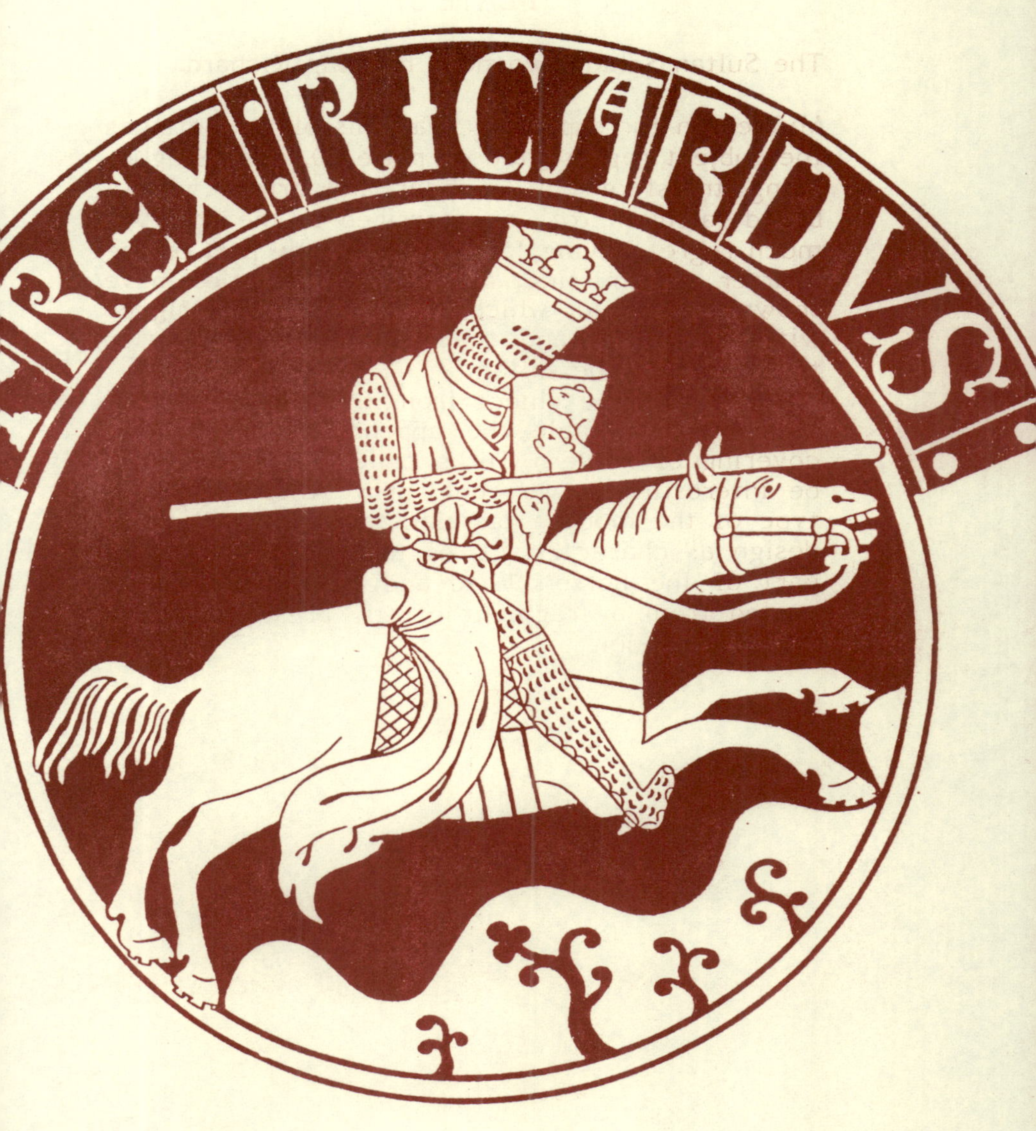
REX · RICARDVS ·

PLATE 31

The Sultan Saladin wounded by King Richard.

My reason for supposing that this plate continues the subject represented on plate 30, is, the figure being transfixed by a spear and armed with a broad falchion, &c., as described in the poem. I much regret having failed to find any part of the quarter tile missing, as it would doubtless have shown the shield, which is described as ensigned with a serpent, and that would have identified this figure as the sultan.

The tassel-like object from the helmet appears to me to resemble the appendage to the head covering of modern Turks called a fez. It would be interesting if we could prove that the prototype of the modern tasseled fez was used in this design as characteristic of the sultan. The lower part of the horse's head and part of the legs I copied from a fragment of tile preserved in the British Museum.

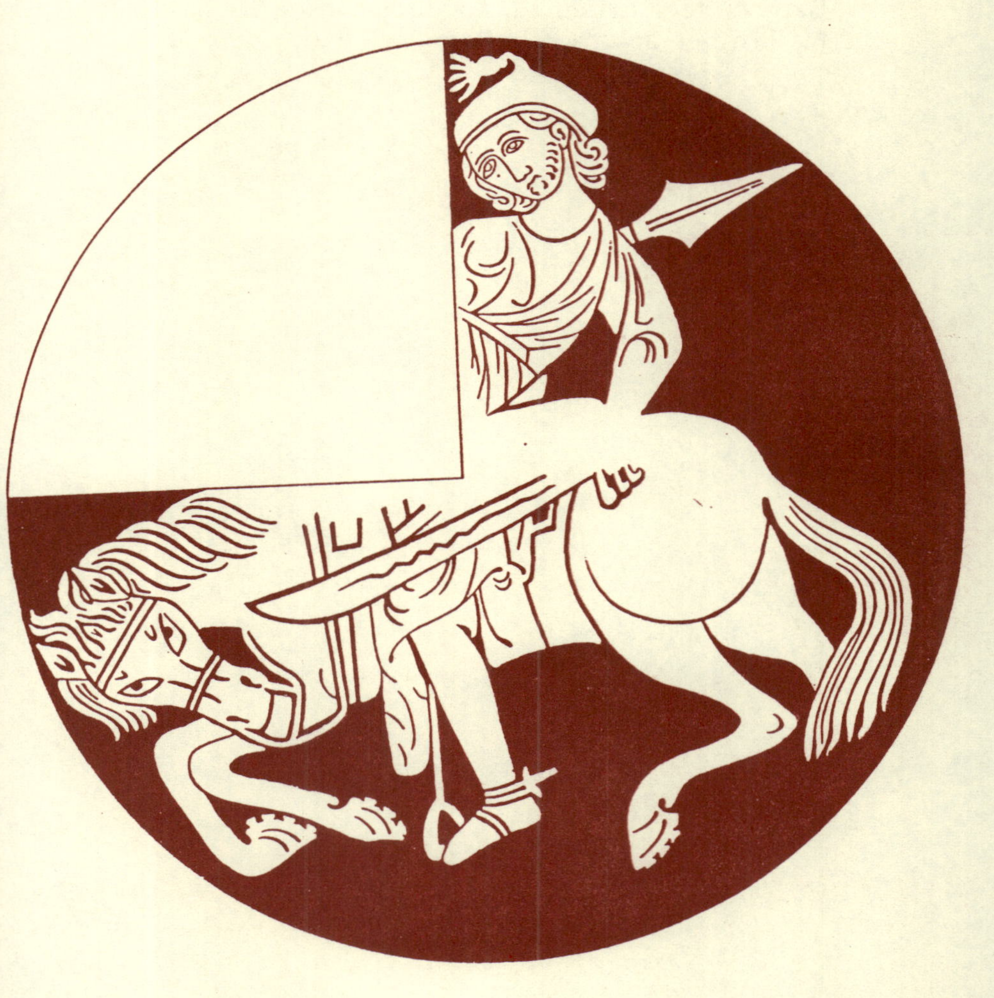

PLATE 32

Messengers bringing a special letter, with the Baron's seal attached, to inform King Richard of his brother John's rebellion.

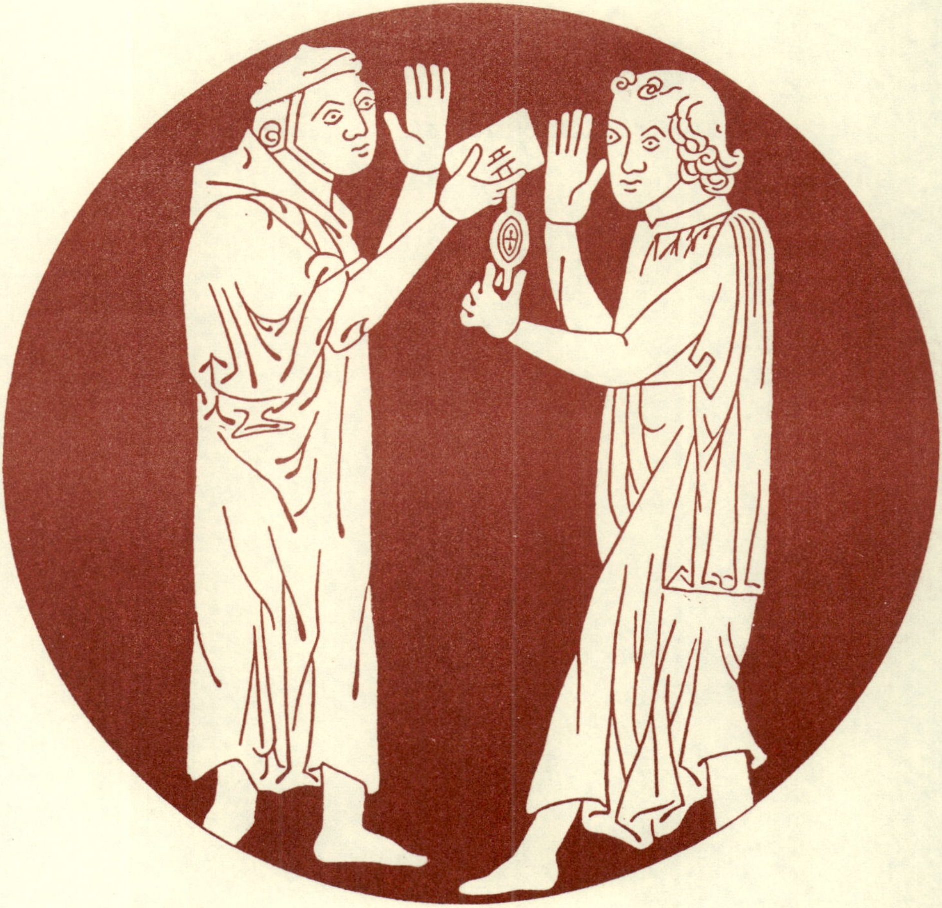

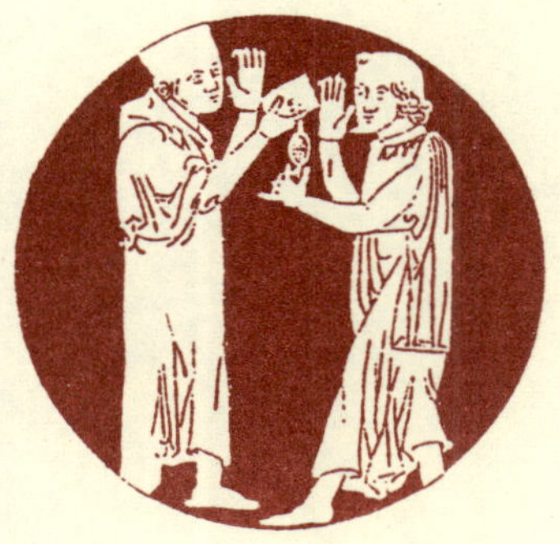

PLATE 33

The knight fighting with a lion.

The attribution of this plate is doubtful.

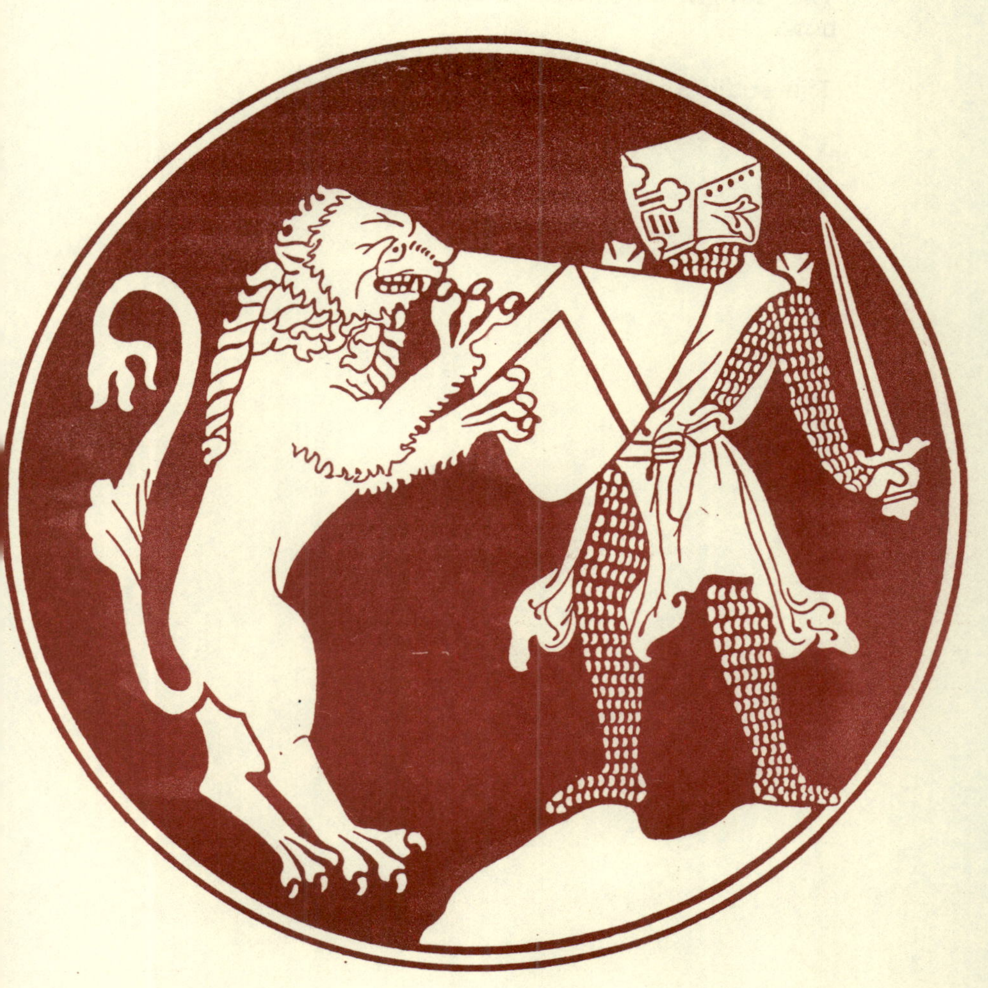

PLATE 34

The knight mounted and armed with a cross-bow.

The subject of this plate is unknown.

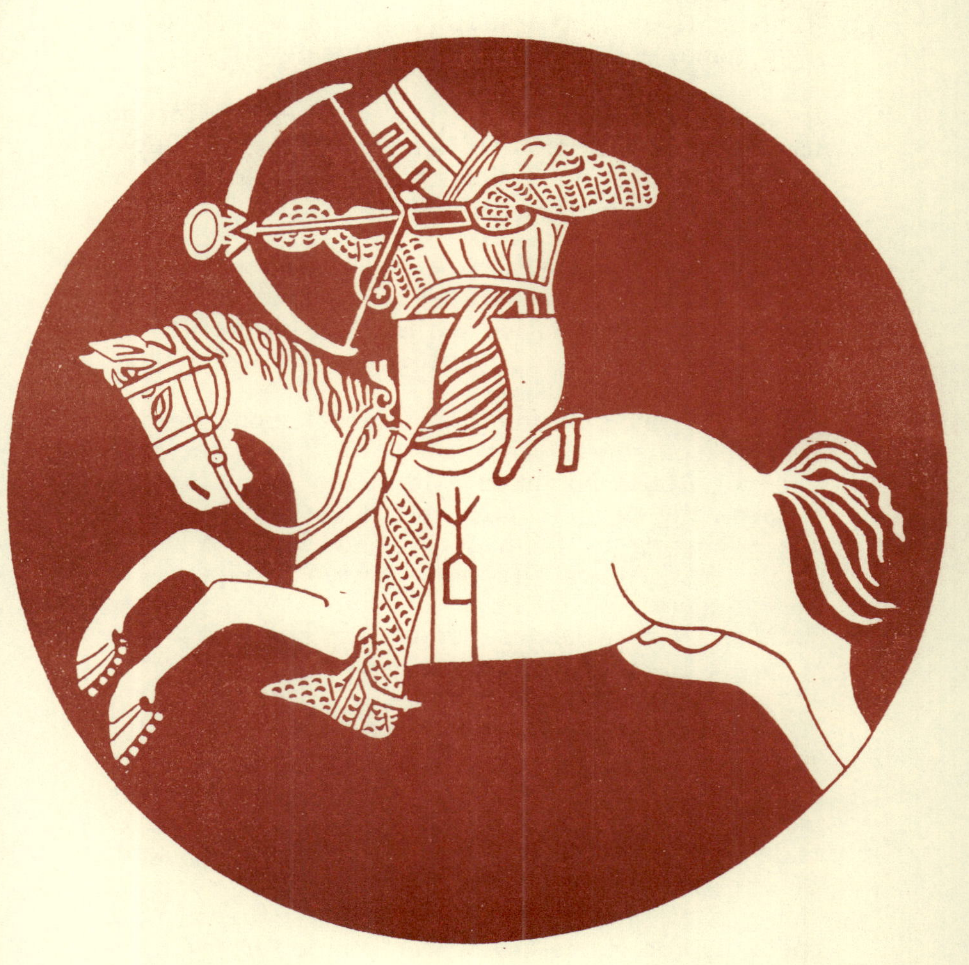

PLATE 35

Represents an Abbot seated, holding a book in his right hand, and in his left a pastoral staff.

It seems probable that it was intended for an ideal representation of Nicholas, Abbot of Hales-Owen. The inscription, with the contractions expanded, may be translated:---

> "This work Abbot Nicholas gave to the Mother of Christ
> That he may flourish without confusion,
> O, Mother grant to Nicholas."

From the terms of the inscription it seems certain that the pavement was laid down during the life-time of Abbot Nicholas who died in 1272. We may suppose the pavement to be not earlier than 1272, the beginning of the reign of Edward I. It seems likely that Abbot Nicholas, wishing to pave the abbey church at Hales-Owen, and having perhaps seen or heard of the pavement at Chertsey, thence obtained as many of the stamps as he could, and that from them and from other stamps obtained from elsewhere, and from some cut on purpose, he had the Hales-Owen tiles made. On this supposition it is possible that the Chertsey pavement was laid down some years earlier than that at Hales-Owen, and thus the later character of some of the designs is accounted for. That some of those tiles which I imagine to have been made specially for Hales-Owen were copied from Chertsey examples is certain. Mr J. R. Holliday's paper on Hales-Owen Abbey was published in the 'Transactions of the Birmingham and Midland Institute,' 1871.

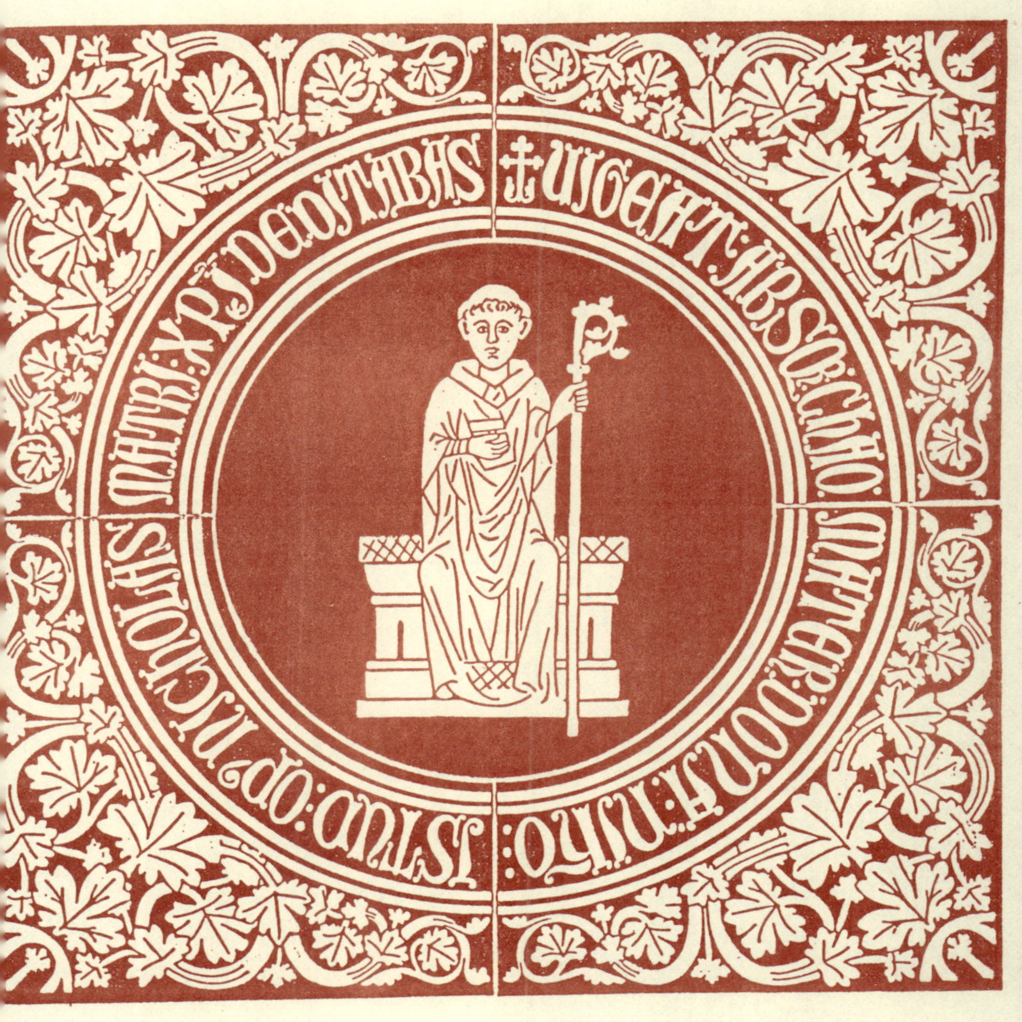

PLATE 36

The inscription may be translated

"Morgan and his attendants return to England."

It is possible that the inscription does not refer to the medallion, the design on which may represent knights bringing Tristan and Ysonde to court from the forest, having been taken into favour again by King Mark.

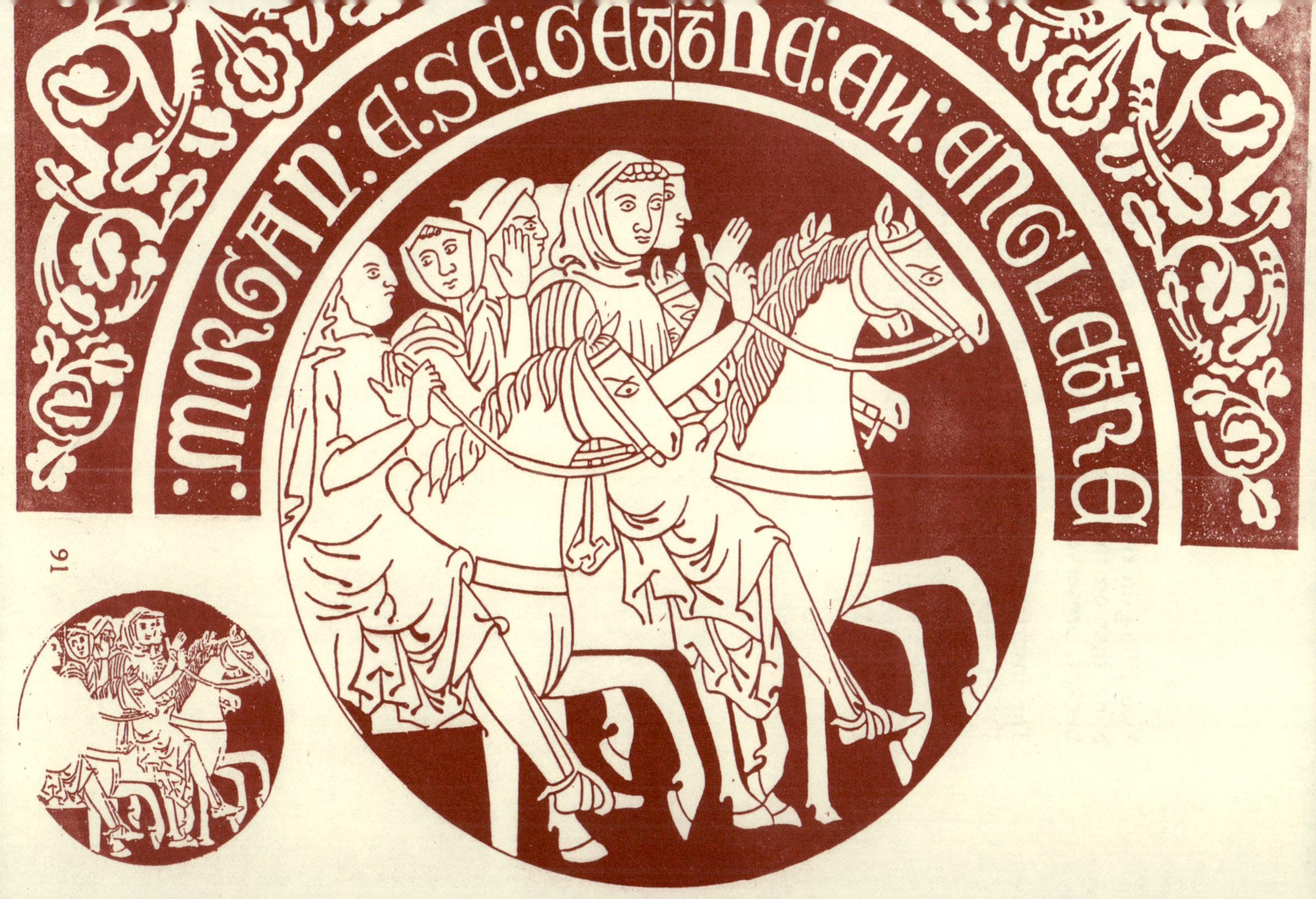

PLATE 37

Two filling-in tiles, stamped with a pattern resembling that on the embroidered mitre of Thomas a Becket, preserved in Sens Cathedral.

The inscription on the border tiles is composed of the so-called pearl letters.

The fragement of medallion represents Brengwain, Ysonde's waiting maid, carrying the cup containing the love potion, prepared by the Queen of Ireland for King Mark.

"The coupe was richeli wrought
Of gold, it was the pin."

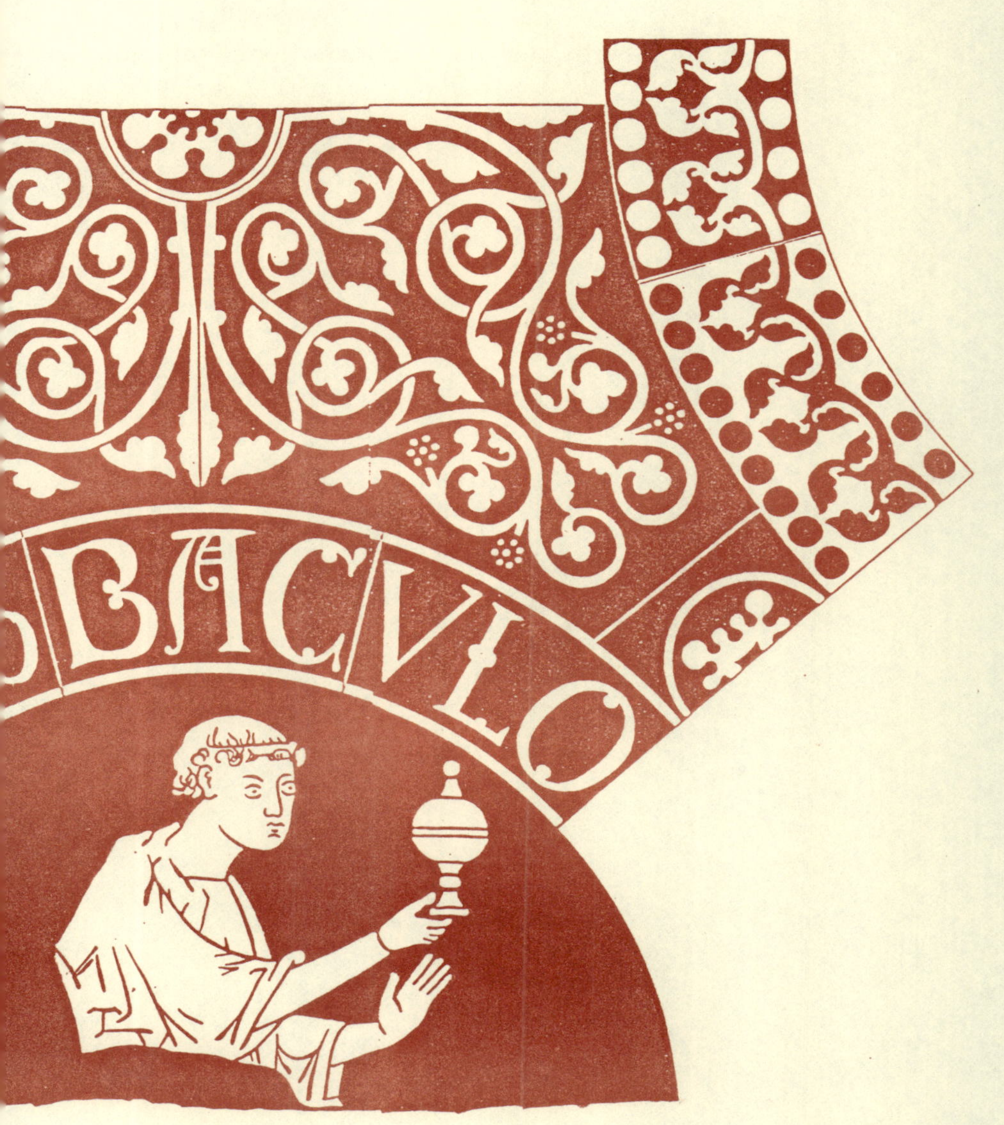
BACVLO

PLATE 38

Filling-in tiles, with designs of conventional foliage.

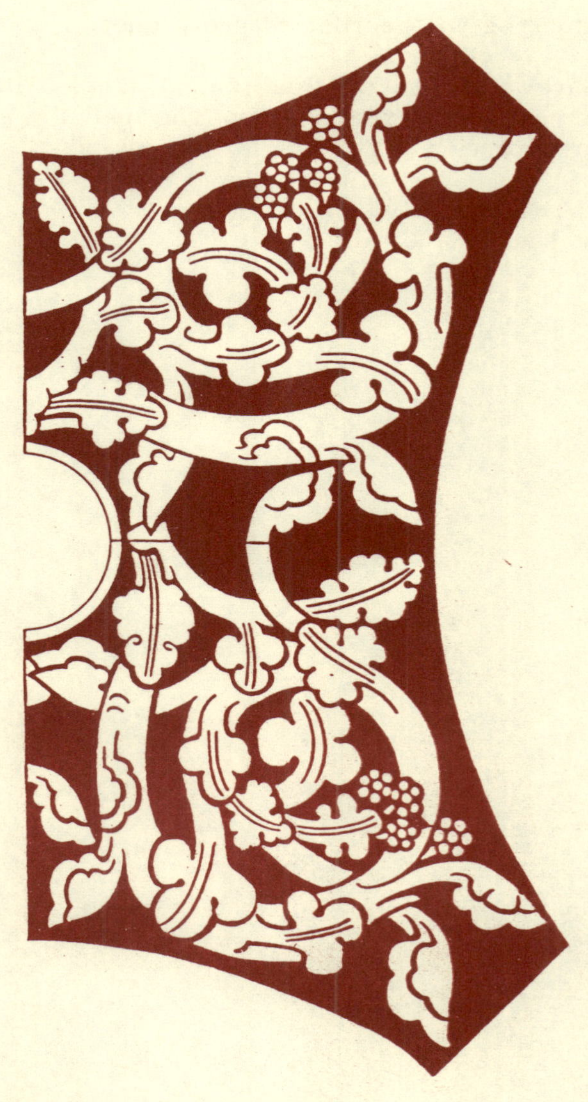

PLATE 39

Frame tile with border of grotesques.

I have drawings of this shaped frame tile with thirteen varieties of border. The medallion represents swearing featly.

> "A forward that began,
> Ther to thai alle sware."

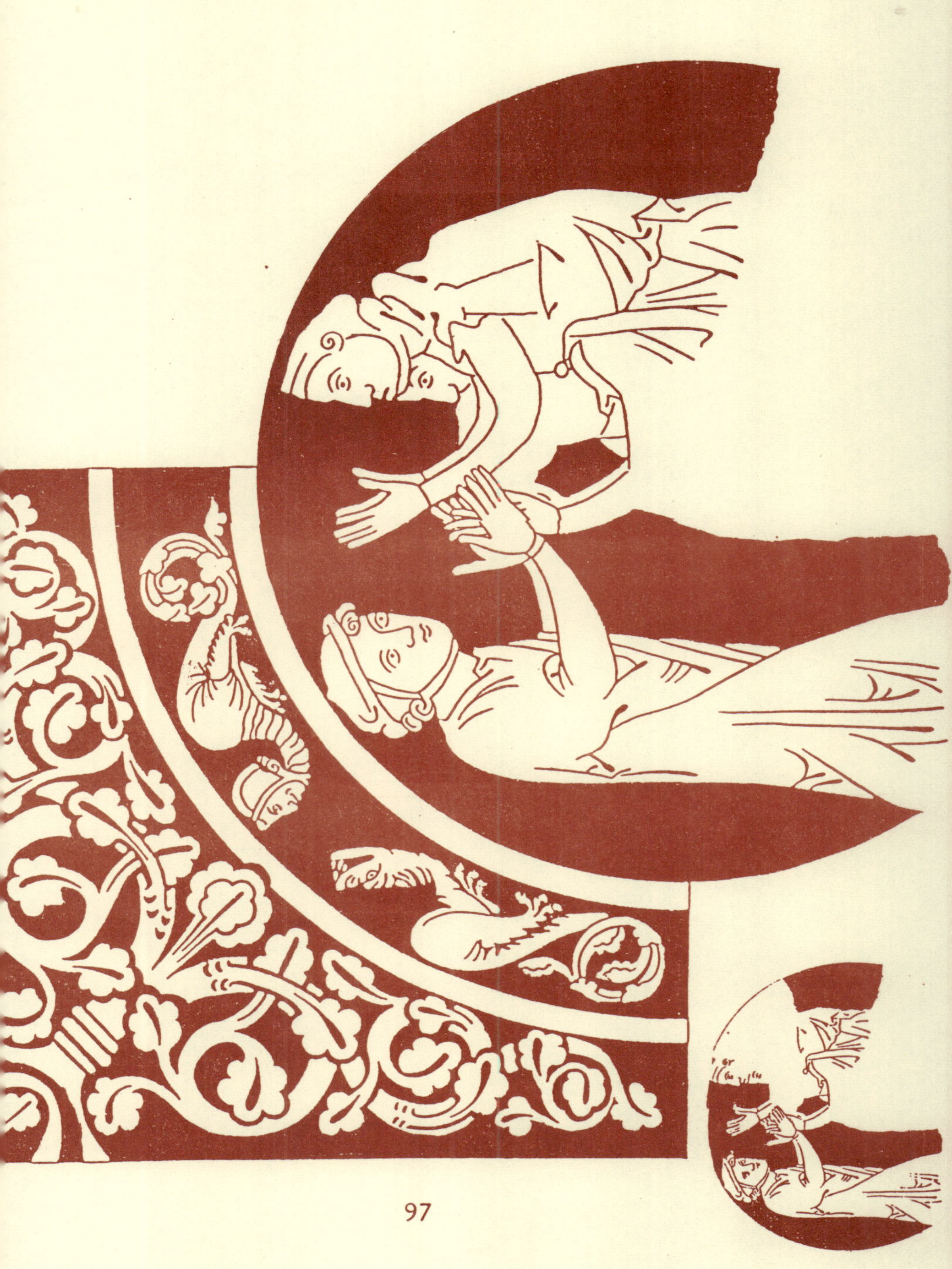

PLATE 40

Tiles used as borders, and also in conjunction with filling-in tiles.

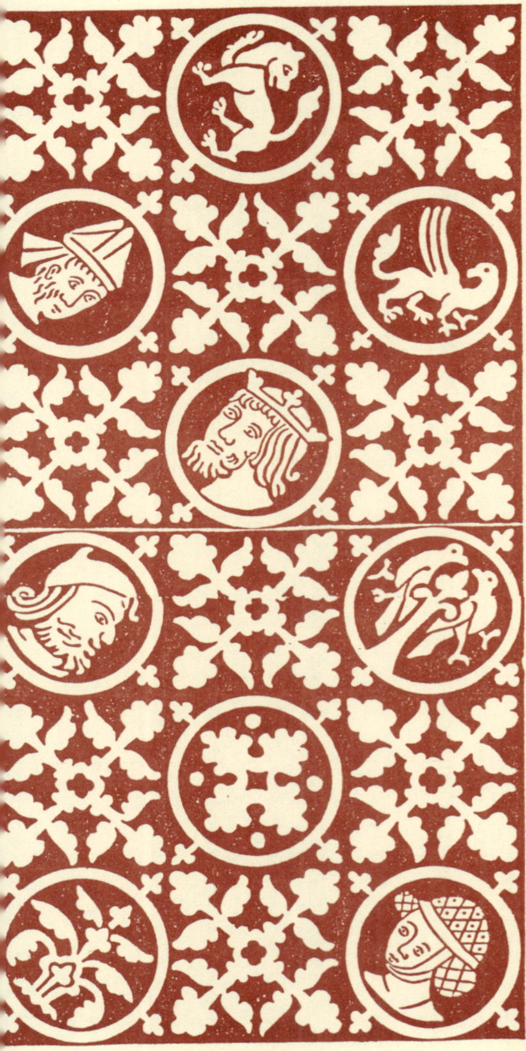

5

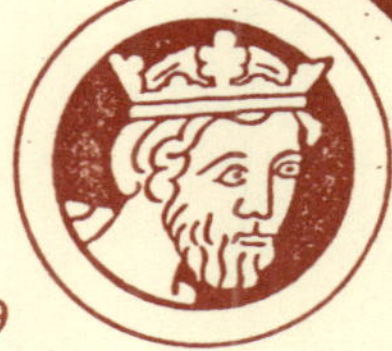

1

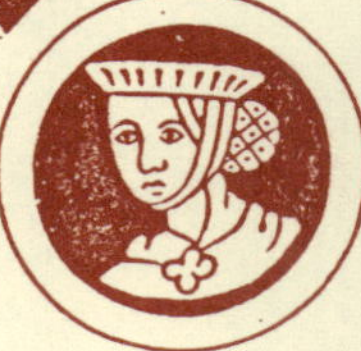

2

NOTES ON ARMOUR DEPICTED ON THE CHERTSEY TILES

By Baron de Cosson.

The most noteworthy points on the drawings are the form of the helm, the long surcoat worn over the hawberk or shirt of mail; the appearance, in two instances, of those defences for the shoulders, termed ailettes; the absence of kneepieces over the mail on the legs; the absence of housings on the horses; the form of the shield; and, in one instance, the representation of banded mail.

From the great seals of the English kings we find the long surcoat first appearing on that of King John, but the headpiece there is very different from those on the tiles. The two seals of his successor, Henry III, show a helmet almost identical with the one most usually depicted on the tiles, and a very similar one is shown on the seal of Edward I. This seal must have been made early in his reign, for by the end of the thirteenth century the helm had assumed a more conical form, as may be seen in the brass of Sir Roger de Trumpington, at Trumpington Church, Cambridge, executed about 1279 - that is in the seventeenth year of the reign of Edward I - and in other documents of that date.

So far as the evidence of the helm goes, the armour on the tiles dates from about 1275.

The seal of Edward I, however, shows the king's horse covered with housings, a fashion which commenced in England at the beginning of his reign. These housings do not appear on any of the tiles, neither are they shown on either of the seals of Henry III.

The ailettes (plate 33) defending the shoulders are first dated on the continent in a manuscript of 1274. Kneepieces followed soon after.

All of these considerations cause me to date the armour on the tiles between 1270 and 1280.

THE ROMANCE POEM OF SIR TRISTREM

In the following summary of Sir Tristrem, I have made use of Sir Walter Scott's running paraphrase in vol. v. of his Poetical Works: "A Metrical Romance of the Thirteenth Century, by Thomas of Erceldoune, called the Rhymer." Herebelow is a facsimile of the commencement of Sir Tristrem. Scott stated that Thomas did not invent the tale of Tristram, but that it laid claim to a much higher antiquity.

I was at (Erceldoune):
With Tomas spak y thare;
Ther herd y rede in roune,
Who Tristrem gat and bare.
Who was king with crown;
And who him forsterd yare;
And who was bold baroun,
As thair elders ware,
· Bi. yere:
Tomas telles in toun,
This auentours as thai ware.
This semly somers day
In winter it is nought sen;
This greues wexen al gray,
That in her time were grene:
So dos this world y say,
Y wis and nought atwene;
The gode bene al oway,
That our elders haue bene,
To abide:
Of a knight is that y mene;
His name is sprong well wide.

The narrator announces that he is about to relate the birth and adventures of Sir Tristrem as they had been communicated to him by Thomas of Ercledoune. After bewailing the degeneracy of the age, he introduces an account of a war between two tribal chiefs, Duke Morgan and Rouland Rise, Lord of Ermonie (Armorica), in which the latter is victorious. A truce having been kept for seven years, Duke Morgan returns to England (see plate 36, inscription "Morgan e se gens tourne en Engleterre") and Rouland Rise goes to the court of Mark, King of Cornwall. A tournament is held at the court, in which Rouland Rise gains the victory, and, at the same time, wins the heart of Princess Blaunche Flour, King Mark's sister. Rouland Rise having been wounded in battle, Blaunche Flour is much distressed, and repairs in private to the chamber of the wounded knight; and Tristrem owes his birth to this stolen interview.

Rouland is informed by a trusty vassal, called Rohand, that Duke Morgan has invaded his dominions in breach of truce. The princess elopes with her lover, who returns to the defence of his land; they arrive safely at a castle belonging to Rohand, where, it would seem, they are married. Duke Morgan comes against Rouland with a great army. A great battle is fought, in which Rouland, after he has achieved prodigies of valour, is defeated, and slain by the Duke by treachery. Blaunche Flour, then in the pains of child-birth, learns of her husband's death. Under these distressing circumstances, a child is born; his mother names him Tristrem, and, after recommending him to the care of Rohand, and bequeathing him a ring as a token of his kinship to King Mark, expires.

Rohand, to secure the safety of his ward, passes him off as his own child, under the anogram of Tramtris. Morgan has gained the absolute lordship over Ermonie, and Rohand pays him constrained and dissembled homage. Tristrem's education for the first fifteen years of his life is described; his skill in minstrelsy, hunting, and knightly games.

A Norwegian vessel arrives, carrying hawks and treasure. Tristrem learns that the captain has challenged anyone to play at chess for a stake of twenty shillings. Rohand and his son and Tristrem go on board the vessel. Tristrem plays with the master at chess, and wins from him six hawks and one hundred pounds (plate 1).

Rohand goes on shore, leaving Tristrem still engaged at chess. The captain, to avoid paying what he has lost, puts to sea with Tristrem. The vessel is sorely "tempest-tost," which the mariners impute to their own injustice; under this impression they pay Tristrem his winnings and put him ashore in an unknown country. Tristrem prays to heaven for protection, and having refreshed himself with some food left by the Norwegians, traverses a forest, in which he meets two palmers, who inform him he is in England. They undertake, for ten shillings, to guide him to the court of King Mark (plate 20).

They meet a party of hunters. Tristrem gives them a lesson in carving the stag and how to blow the mort, or tokening. This new science is communicated to King Mark, who is highly delighted with so important a discovery. Tristrem is brought before King Mark, to whom he gives an account of his education; but as the name of Rohand, our hero's supposed father, was unknown to the king, he does not discover his nephew in the young huntsman.

Tristrem partakes of a royal feast. The introduction of a minstrel after the feast gives Tristrem an opportunity of displaying his skill on the harp, in which the Cornish musician yields him the palm. He becomes a great favourite with King Mark (plate 2).

The tale returns to Rohand, who, desperate at the loss of his foster-son, searches for him over various countries, without even renewing his tattered clothing, until he meets one of the palmers who conducted Tristrem to the court of King Mark, who, at Rohand's request, guides him there.

When Rohand arrives at the castle he is refused entrance by the porter on account of his mean dress (plates 3 and 4). Having bribed him by a gold ring, he allows him to pass, but the usher also has to be bribed by another gold ring before he will bring him to Tristrem, who at first fails to regognize him in his tattered garments. An explanation takes place, and Tristrem, shocked by his mistake, introduces Rohand to King Mark as his father, who orders him a bath and to be richly attired. Rohand tells the King the secret of Tristrem's birth, and produces the token of the ring bequeathed by his mother on her death bed. Mark receives Tristrem as his nephew, and kisses him (plate 5). He is congratulated and kissed by all the knights and ladies of the court (plate 6).

Tristrem becomes urgent to learn the particulars of his father's death. Rohand tells him of the tragic fate of both his parents - through Duke Morgan's treachery. Tristrem announces to the king his intention to go to Ermonie to avenge his father's death (plate 8). Mark dissuades his nephew from so dangerous an attempt (plate 8), but at length gives his consent, and bestows upon him the honour of knighthood. Tristrem resolves to go in disguise to Duke Morgan's court. He arrives there while they are at table, at the head of fifteen knights, each of whom carries a boar's head as a present. An ambiguous greeting from Tristrem leads the Duke to demand his name and business. Tristrem declares himself, and, at the conclusion of an angrey parley, Morgan strikes him with his fist (plate 9). Tristrem draws his sword, and, at that instant, Rohand arrives with his army. An engagement ensues, in which Morgan is slain and his followers routed. Sir Tristrem recovers his paternal dominions, which he confers upon Rohand, to be held of himself as liege lord (plate 10). Our hero takes leave of Sir Rohand and returns to Cornwall.

On Tristrem's arrival in Cornwall he finds the land in dismay, on account of a tribute demanded of Mark by the King of Ireland. The nature of the tribute is explained as the yearly payment of three hundred pounds in gold, as many of coined silver, and as many of tin; and every fourth year of three hundred children (plate 11). Mouaunt, the Irish Ambassador, is engaged in demanding the tribute when Tristrem arrives from Ermonie. Mark explains to his nephew that the demand is utterly unjust. The matter is discussed in the council of the nation, where Tristrem undertakes, upon his knighthood, to defend the freedom of Cornwall. Tristrem delivers in person to Moraunt a declaration that no tribute was due. Moraunt retorts by giving the lie to Tristrem, and they exchange gages of battle. They sail to a small island to decide the combat. Tristrem sets his boat adrift, saying, in answer to Moraunt's question why he does so, that one would be sufficient to bring back the victor. In the encounter, Tristrem is desperately wounded in the thigh (plate 12) but Moraunt has his skull cleft, a broken piece of Tristrem's sword remaining in the wound (plate 13). Tristrem exults in having slain the mirror of Ireland. The attendants remove Moraunt's body (plate 14), and Tristrem returns to Cornwall and presents his sword at the altar. (Note, the Black Book of the Exchequer mentions this item "Ensem Tristrami," and the connection of Tristrem's sword with the regalia may have been a symbol of the crown rights of Cornwall. The sword was preserved in the Tower Treasury from 1365 to 1649, when most of the crown jewels were dispersed)... Tristrem's wound becomes worse, and the stench from its gangrenous state drives everyone away, except his faithful servant, Gouvernayl.

Tristrem, forsaken by everyone, bewails his lot to King Mark, and asks him for a ship so that he may leave the country of Cornwall (plate 15). Mark grants his request, and he embarks with his sole attendant, Gouvernayl. He is nine weeks at sea; the wind at length drives him to the haven of Dublin. Learning that he is in Ireland, and remembering that Moraunt, whom he had slain, was brother to the queen of that country, he again assumes the name of Tramtris. The wounded man's skill in minstrelsy is reported to the queen, a lady celebrated for her skill in medicine.

"She sent him a plaster kene
To cast the stink oway."

The queen comes to visit Tristrem (plate 16), who maintains his assumed name and the character of a merchant plundered and robbed by pirates. His skill in music, and at chess, and tables, astonishes the queen. She undertakes his cure, and restores him to health by a medicated bath. His skill in music and games occasions his being frequently called to court; and he becomes instructor to the Princess Isonde in minstrelsy and poetry, as well as chess and other games. Sir Tristrem's health being restored, and the education of Ysonde completed, our hero becomes desirous of returning to Britain. The queen unwillingly grants his request, with some reflections upon the ingratitude of foreigners. King Mark receives him joyfully, and enquires how his wound has been cured. Tristrem informs the king of the kindness of the sister of Moraunt, and also praises the beauty and accomplishments of Ysonde. The king offers to make Tristrem his heir if he will bring Ysonde to Cornwall. Tristrem undertakes the enterprise and sails to Dublin, accompanied by fifteen knights. He sends rich presents to the king, queen, and princess by messengers, who return full of the praises of Ysonde's beauty, and relate that the people of Ireland are in great alarm at the approach of a dragon, which had done so much mischief that a proclamation had been made offering the hand of the princess to him who should slay the monster. Tristrem proposes the adventure to his knights, who decline to undertake it. He goes on shore himself well-mounted and armed, and after a fearful combat slays the dragon (plates 17 and 18). He cuts out the dragon's tongue and places it "in his hose next his hide," but is soon, by the subtle operation of the poison, deprived of his senses. Meanwhile, the king's steward chances to pass by, believing Tristrem dead, he cuts off the dragon's head, carries it to the court, and demands the hand of the princess. Ysonde and the queen, not believing the steward, resolve to visit the place where the battle had been fought. They find the steed and arms of Tristrem, and at length Tristrem himself. Being restored by the queen, Tristrem vindicates his right to the victory by producing the tongue, and offers to make good his story upon the person of the steward in single combat (plate 19). As he calls himself a merchant, Ysonde expresses her regret that he is not a knight. The queen and Ysonde, admiring the bravery and handsome figure of Tristrem, conduct him in person to a bath. The queen goes to fetch a drink of "main," and meanwhile Ysonde becomes suspicious that the stranger is Tristrem. In searching for something to confirm this conjecture she examines his sword, which she finds to be broken. By comparing it with the fragment taken from Moraunt's skull, she discovers that the owner of the weapon has slain her kinsman. She upbraids Tristrem with his slaughter, and rushes upon him with his own sword. The queen, on her return, joins in her resentment. The arrival of the king saves Tristrem from being slain in the bath. Tristrem defends himself as having slain Moraunt in a fair fight, and pleads his services towards her as Tramtris, and the good report he had made of her charms to King Mark, and finally opens his embassy. Upon the formal request of Tristrem that his uncle should marry Ysonde, it is agreed that she should be sent under his escort to Cornwall. The steward relinquishes his claim as soon as he learns that his antagonist is Tristrem, and is put in prison by the king at the request of the princess (plates 20 and 21). At their departure the queen gives Brengwain, a lady who attended on Ysonde, a powerful philtre for Mark and his bride to partake of on the evening of their marriage (plate 37). While at sea the wind becomes contrary, and they have to use the oars. Tristrem exerts himself in rowing, and Ysonde calls for drink to refresh him. Brengwain inadvertently presents the cup which contains the love potion, and Tristrem and Ysonde partake of it. The consequence is a passion between them, which proves the source of all their misfortunes. The ship reaches Cornwall after a fortnight's sail, and Ysonde is married to King Mark.

At length, Tristrem is banished from Cornwall through his intercourse with the queen. He enters into the service of Triamour, King of Wales, who is unjustly attacked by Urgan, a neighbouring prince, who lays waste his country. Triamour promises Tristrem a grant of his Welsh dominions if he can recover them from the enemy. Tristrem and Urgan join battle, and at length meet in single combat. After a desperate fight, Tristrem is the victor.

The fame of Tristrem's exploits reaching the court of Cornwall, Mark invites him back. His uncle becomes reconciled to him, and gives him the office of grand steward; but all his efforts are unable to counterbalance the power of the love potion. The amours of Tristrem and Ysonde resume, and are again discovered, and they are banished from King Mark's dominions. The lovers fly to a forest and enjoy their freedom. Tristrem hunts with his favourite greyhound Houdain (plate 22), and bow "qui-ne-faut" (plate 23). King Mark, while hunting in the forest, discovers them sleeping together, but with a drawn sword laid between them; from this circumstance he argues that no undue communication subsisted between them. His obsequious train assent to this reasoning. The king sends a party of knights to conduct them to court (plate 36), and he is once more fully reconciled to them both.

Tristrem being again discovered by the king too intimate with Ysonde, has to fly from court, leaving her behind. During his banishment, he engages in most desperate enterprises. He traverses Spain where he slays three giants. From Spain he goes to Ermonie, where he is joyfully received by his vassals, the sons of his old tutor, Rohand. They offer to restore to him his hereditary dominions, which he declines to receive. Tristrem arrives in Brittany, where he assists the duke of that land in his wars. By our hero's valour, the contest is soon ended. Tristrem is introduced to the duke's lovely daughter. This lady bears the same name as the Queen of Cornwall; but, for distinction, is called Ysonde with the white hand. Tristrem sings of the beauty of the Queen of Cornwall, and the Princess of Brittany, having the same name, is led to believe him her lover, and communicates her mistake to her father. The duke offers Tristrem his daughter's hand. They are betrothed and married, but live unhappily.

Queen Ysonde, feeling very lonely and wretched

through Tristrem's absence, distracts herself by singing the songs he had taught her (plate 24).

Tristrem, after a quarrel, renounces his wife, declares his intention of returning to his first love, and goes to Cornwall in disguise. Brengwain is prevailed upon to procure him an interview with the queen in her chamber at night. Tristrem, being disguised as a court fool, reveals himself by singing her songs (plate 25).

Brengwain accuses Tristrem of cowardice, and he replies by desiring that a tournament might be proclaimed, in which he may vindicate his reputation. During the tournament, Tristrem, with the assistance of Ganhardin, slays and routs all that come against him; his "courtly tale-carriers are shamefully worsted." Tristrem returns to Brittany, where he meets a young knight of the same name who has sought him for a long time, and who begs his assistance, a knight having deprived him of his lady. The ravisher, with seven brothers and seven other knights, are to escort their prize that very day to some place of security; the suppliant knight proposes to his namesake to assist him in her rescue. Tristrem readily assents. The two knights arm and prepare for battle; they attack the party of ravishers on a "lee beside a forest." Tristrem the younger is soon slain; our hero avenges his death by slaying the fifteen knights. In this battle he receives an arrow in his old wound.

(At this point the Auchinlick manuscript used by Sir Walter Scott ends. The remaining pages have been torn away. The conclusion that follows is based on the French Metrical Romance.)

Tristrem, desperately wounded by the arrow, is carried to his castle, but every remedy is tried in vain. The gangrene becomes daily worse, and can be cured by none but Ysonde of Cornwall, to whom Tristrem despatches Ganhardin, his wife's brother, with his ring as a token, directing him to inform the queen of his extremity. He tells him to take two sails, one white and the other black, the former to be used on his return should Ysonde be on board, and the latter if his embassy should be unsuccessful. Ysonde, his wife, overhears this conversation, and resolves to be avenged of Tristrem for his infidelity.

Queen Ysonde agrees to accompany Ganhardin and disguises herself as a man. They approach the coast of Brittany displaying the white sail (plate 26).

Ysonde of Brittany, fired with jealousy, hastens to her husband to tell him that Ganhardin's ship is in sight. He asks the colour of the sail; she informs him black as pitch, whereupon he falls back in despair and dies. When Ysonde arrives and learns of her lover's death, she rushes to the castle where the corpse is laid out (plate 27), and expires from grief beside him.

THE ROMANCE POEM OF RICHARD COEUR DE LION

The romance poem of Richard Coeur de Lion, in vol. ii of Henry Weber's "Metrical Romances of the Thirteenth, Fourteenth and Fifteenth Centuries," Edinburgh, 1810, is very readable and amusing. It begins:---

"Lord Jesus, King of Glorie,
Such grace and vyctorie
Thou sente to King Rychard,
That never was found coward!
It is good to here in jest
Of his prowesse and conqueste."

That history is not followed is very evident from the introductory chapter, which informs us that King Richard's father, King Henry, consents, at the request of his barons, to marry the fairest woman alive. Messengers are sent to find her, and they meet a vessel, in which the King of Antioch and his daughter had sailed for the very purpose of going to England. They are conducted to London.

Then asked he that lady bright:
"What hyghtest thow my swete wyght?"
"Cassodorien, withouten lesyng,"
Thus answered sche the kyng.

The marriage is celebrated. The queen swoons at the elevation of the host. Three children, Richard, John, and Topyas are born. The queen being forced to remain at a sacrament, flies through the roof of a church, and takes her two youngest children with her. John is dropped, and in falling fractures his thigh bone. King Henry dies and leaves his crown to his son Richard.

CHAPTER 2. King Richard is crowned. He proclaims a tournament. In three disguises he jousts with his knights to discover the worthiest among them. He chooses Sir Thomas Multon and Sir Fulk Doyly, reveals himself to them, and engages them to accompany him, in the guise of palmers, to the Holy Land.

This incident is represented on a medallion, but is too imperfect to publish. The king carries a sergeant's mace or sceptre.

CHAPTER 3. Richard and his two knights visit the Holy Land. On their return through Germany they are, by a minstrel, betrayed to the king, and imprisoned by him. Richard, challenged by Ardour the king's son, kills him by a blow. He is condemned to death, but reprieved by Margery the king's daughter. His private intercourse with her is discovered; and by the advice of Sir Eldryd, a lion is brought into his prison to devour him. Richard, however, kills it by pulling out its heart (plate 28).

The scene with the lion is described in the poem thus:---

"With that com the jaylere
And other two with him in fere,
And the lyon hem among,
Hys pawes was both scharpe and long,
Rychard cried, 'Help, Jesu!'
The lyon made a great venu,
And wolde have him al to-rent.
King Rychard bethought hym that tyde,
What it was best, and to hym sterte,
In at hys throte hys arme he gerte:
Rent out the herte with hys hand,
Lungges, and lyvere, and al that he fand.
The lyoun fel ded to the grounde.
Rychard had neyther wemme ne wounde;
He knelyd down in that place,

And thanked God off his grace,
That hym kepte fro schame and harme.
He took the herte al so warme,
And brought it into the halle,
Before the king and hys men alle.
The kyng at meet sat on des,
With dukes, and erles, prowde in pres.
The saler on the table stood,
Rychard prest out al the blood,
And wette the herte in the salt,
(The kyng and al hys men behalt)
Withouten bred the herte he eet.
The kyng wonderyd, and sayd skeet:
'I wis, as I undyrstande can,
This is a devyl and no man,
That has my stronge lyoun slawe,
The herte out of hys body drawe,
And has it eeten with good wylle!
He may be callyd, be right skylle,
Kyng i-chrystenyd off most renown,
Stronge Rychard Coer de Lyoun!' "

CHAPTER 8. Richard begins his operations against Acre. The Saracens assault the camp while King Richard lies ill in his tent.

"Kyng Rychard was syke tho'
Al Crystendom to mekyl woo!
He might hym nought off hys bed ster,
Though hys pavyloun had be on fer."

He is cured and longs for pork, which is not to be procured.

"Affter pork he was alonged,
But, though hys men scholde be hongyd,
They ne myghte, in that cuntree,
For gold, ne sylvyr, ne no monee,
No pork fynde, take, ne gete."

An old knight recommends that a Saracen be killed and cooked, which is done (plate 29).

"The sothe to saye, at wurdes fewe,
Slayn and soden was the hethene schrewe,
Beffore the kyng it was forth brought.
Quod hys men, 'Lord we have pork brought,
Etes, and soupes off the browys swote,
Thorowgh grace off God it schall be your boote.'
Beffore Kyng Rychard karff a knyght;
He eete faster than he karffe myght;
And whenne he hadde eeten inowgh,
Hys folk hem turned away and lowgh."

Being much refreshed by his meal, Richard sallies forth, and in an engagement makes a great slaughter of Saracens; returns feeble and faint, and bids the cook being him the head of the swine for his supper.

"The hed off that ilke swyn,
That I off eet (the cook he bad).
Quod the cook, 'That hed I ne have.'
Thenne sayde the kyng, 'so God me save,
But I see the hed off that swyn,
For sothe thou schalt lesen thyn!' "

The cook fetched the head, and

"He fel on his knees and made a cry:
'Loo, here the hed! my lord, mercy!'
The swarte vys when the kyng seeth,
Hys blacke berd and whyte teeth,
How hys lyppys grenned wyde:
'What devyl is this?' the kyng cryde:
And gan to laughe as he wer wood,
'What, is Sarezynys flesch thus good?' "

And added that there need be no want of food as

long as Saracens could be obtained.

The first chapter of the second part of the poem begins:---

"Merye is, in the tyme off May,
Whenne foulis synge in her lay.
Floures on appyl trees, and perye,
Small foules synge merye.
Ladyes strowe here bowres,
With rede roses, and lylye floures."

The fourth chapter describes how King Richard beseiges Babylon. The Sultan Saladin offers to fight Richard in a general battle, which he accepts. A steed is presented to Richard by Saladin, of which he is warned by an angel. Saladin, having been badly wounded by Richard, flies (plates 30 and 31).

"Rychard was rychely begoo,
From the crest unto the too.
He was armyd wondyr weel,
And al with plates off good steel;
And ther aboven an hawberk;
A schafft wrought off trusty work.
On hys shuldre a schield off steel.
With three lupardes wrought ful weel.

"For grete pryde, without lesyng,
  A brod fawchoun to hym he bar,
  For he thought that he wolde thar,
Have slayn Kyng Rychard with treasoun.

"He strook the fiend that undyr hym yede,
And gaff the sawdon a dynt off dede.
In his blasoun, verrament,
Was i-paynted a serpent.
With the speere that Rychard heeld,

He bar him thorwgh undyr the scheeld.
None off hys armes myghte laste,
Brydyl and peytrel al to brast;
Hys gerth, and hys stiropes alsoo;
The mere to the grounde gan goo.
Mawgry hym he garte hym stoupe,
Bakward ovyr hys mere's croupe;
The feet toward the fyrmament.
Behynd the Sawdon the spere out went."

In Chapter 6 King Richard hears of his brother John's rebellion in England (plate 32).

"Thereafftyr in a lytyl stounde,
Come messengers off mekyl mound;
The Bisschop of Chestre was that on,
That othir the Abbot of Seynt Albon.
That brought him letters speciele,
Aselyd with the baroun's sele,
That tolden him, hys brother Ihon
Wolde docorowne hym anon,
At the Pask, be comen dome,
But he the rather wolde come home."

The manuscript concludes:

"Kyng Rychard, doughty off hand
Turnyd homeward to Yngeland,
Kyng Rychard reynyd here
No more but ten yere.
Sythe he was schot, alas!
In Castle Gayland ther he was.
Thus endyd Rychard our kyng.
God give us alle good endyng,
And hys soule reste and roo,
And our soules whenne we com thertoo!"

-§-

Also published by Llanerch:

TALIESIN POEMS
translated by Meirion Pennar

A HISTORY OF THE
KINGS OF ENGLAND
by Florence of Worcester
translated by J. Stephenson

THE LEGENDARY XII HIDES
OF GLASTONBURY
by Ray Gibbs

THE MYSTICAL WAY
AND THE ARTHURIAN QUEST
by Derek Bryce

ARTHUR AND THE BRITONS
IN WALES AND SCOTLAND
by W. F. Skene

From booksellers.

For a complete list, write to:
LLANERCH ENTERPRISES,
Felinfach, Lampeter, Dyfed,
SA48 8PJ